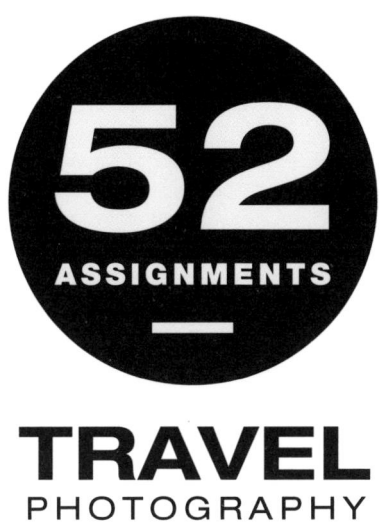

TRAVEL
PHOTOGRAPHY

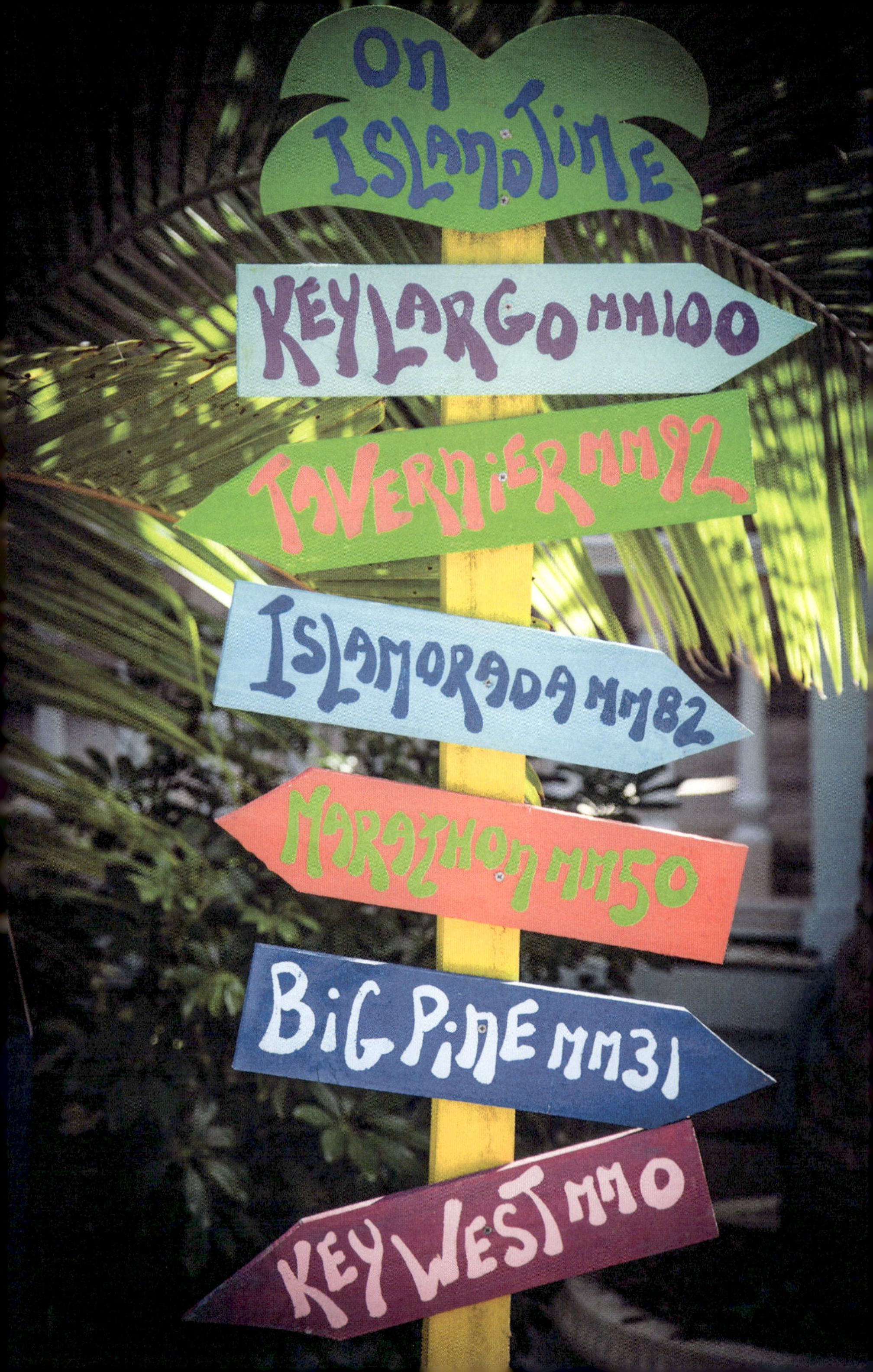

On Island Time
KEY LARGO MM100
TAVERNIER MM92
ISLAMORADA MM82
MARATHON MM50
BiG PINE MM31
KEY WEST MM0

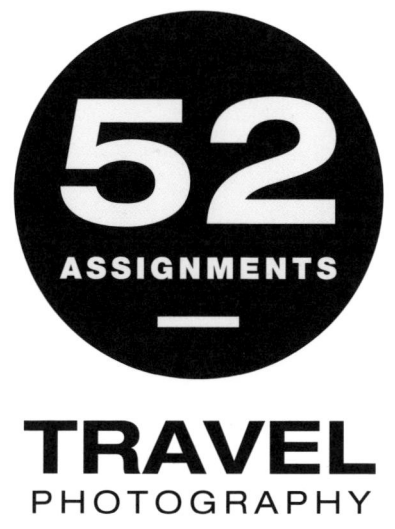

52
ASSIGNMENTS
—

TRAVEL
PHOTOGRAPHY

ANTONY ZACHARIAS

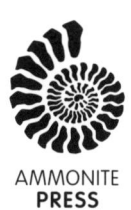

AMMONITE
PRESS

ASSIGNMENTS

Tick off your completed projects

☐ 01 REFLECTIONS 8

☐ 02 SIGHTS UNSEEN 10

☐ 03 TRAVELOGUE 12

☐ 04 ALTERNATIVE POSTCARD 16

☐ 05 THE IMAGE THAT NEVER SLEEPS 18

☐ 06 ADMIRE THE VIEW 22

☐ 07 MEET THE LOCALS 24

☐ 08 DETAILS, DETAILS 26

☐ 09 IMAGINARY JOURNEY 28

☐ 10 SUNSEEKER 30

☐ 11 LIFE IN MOTION 32

☐ 12 A SPLASH OF COLOR 34

☐ 13 THEMES 36

☐ 14 TRANSPORT OF DELIGHT 38

☐ 15 CAFE SOCIETY 42

☐ 16 EAT LIKE A LOCAL 44

☐ 17 BRIGHT LIGHTS, BIG CITY 46

☐ 18 CULTURE CLUB 50

☐ 19 TRAVEL PATTERNS 52

☐ 20 A MYSTERIOUS STRANGER 54

☐ 21 CRYSTAL BALL 56

☐ 22 YOU'VE BEEN FRAMED 58

☐ 23 CLIMB ANY MOUNTAIN 60

☐ 24 SILHOUETTED 62

☐ 25 IN THE SHADOWS 66

☐ 26 SIGNPOSTING 68

ASSIGNMENT KEY

Each assignment has symbols showing the type of tasks involved.

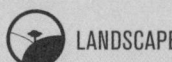 LANDSCAPE 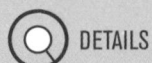 DETAILS 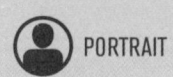 PORTRAIT

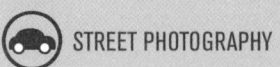 STREET PHOTOGRAPHY 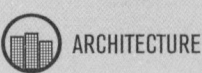 ARCHITECTURE

☐	27	GO WITH THE FLOW	70	☐	40	MONOTONE MEMORIES	98
☐	28	ROAD TRIP	72	☐	41	KEEP IT SIMPLE	100
☐	29	RAIN OR SHINE	74	☐	42	PICTURE POSTCARD	102
☐	30	ADRENALINE RUSH	76	☐	43	SUITS TO SAREES	104
☐	31	ARCHITECTURE TOUR	78	☐	44	MOVE YOUR FEET	106
☐	32	ON SAFARI	80	☐	45	TRAVEL TEXTURES	108
☐	33	READ ALL ABOUT IT	82	☐	46	TRAVEL JOURNALIST	110
☐	34	MAP IT OUT	86	☐	47	ALL IN A DAY'S WORK	114
☐	35	THE SPEED OF THE CITY	88	☐	48	AMID THE RUINS	116
☐	36	OPPOSITES ATTRACT	90	☐	49	A GRAND CANYON	118
☐	37	CITY WALLS	92	☐	50	ROAD TO NOWHERE	120
☐	38	MYSTERY TOUR	94	☐	51	ALPHABET CITY	122
☐	39	KITSCH IS COOL	96	☐	52	CONQUER THE WORLD	124

ASSIGNMENT JOURNAL

Use the journal spaces throughout the book to keep a record of your experimental assignments and images.

INTRODUCTION

Photography is truly amazing. It allows you to tell a story, provoke ideas, and convey mood and emotion, all without the need for any words. When you combine this with the excitement of traveling—of exploring and seeing countless new things—you have the potential to capture stunning images that go far beyond simply showing where you were in the world.

However, travel photography can be tricky. Although we can get to distant and exotic places with relative ease, once we arrive it can sometimes be a little overwhelming from a photographic point of view. There is such a wide variety of new subject matter around us that it can be difficult to know where to start with your camera. The problem is, randomly pointing and clicking at everything you see will not produce the best photographs of your travels. In fact, the opposite is true, and this is where the questions begin: How do you choose your subject matter? How do you portray it? What story do you want to share with your audience?

The assignments in this book are designed to help you answer these questions, and more, so you can focus on exploration and enjoyment, and immersing yourself in your chosen destination and culture, rather than being distracted about what to photograph. Each assignment will encourage you to think a little more about where you are and what makes that place unique, be it the people you meet or the sights and smells that you encounter.

Whether you concentrate on details, people, architecture, or stunning landscapes, these assignments will make you look harder and see with more focus. The challenges will encourage you to explore, observe, create, and enjoy, so you return home with a wide range of interesting and exciting images that not only capture the essence of your travels, but also take you on a fun photographic journey.

Antony Zacharias

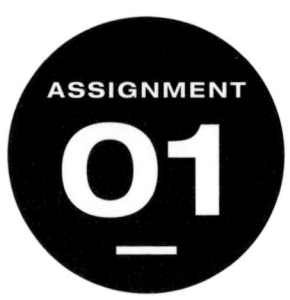

TECHNIQUE

- Consider your composition and how you want to use the reflection. Using a reflection to divide a scene in half can deliver a strong and powerful symmetry.

- Explore different angles to create an interesting reflected photograph, but take care not to include yourself or your camera in the shot.

- The angle of the light—whether it's the sun or an artificial light source—will affect the intensity of the reflections.

REFLECTIONS

Reflections are all around you. No matter where you are you will often see mirrored views from a wide variety of shiny, reflective surfaces, such as glass windows and doors, puddles, water, metal, or gloss-painted objects.

Reflected views can provide you with an interesting way of seeing things, as they create an alternative version of your surroundings. Compositionally, they can be used in a range of ways, such as creating patterns and symmetry (see Assignment 19), or they can challenge your viewer's perception of a scene by distorting reality and making things appear more abstract.

Your assignment here is to create a captivating image where reflections are the main focus. Think about how you want to use the reflections: whether they are there to mirror a beautiful scene or to confuse your viewer about how things really are.

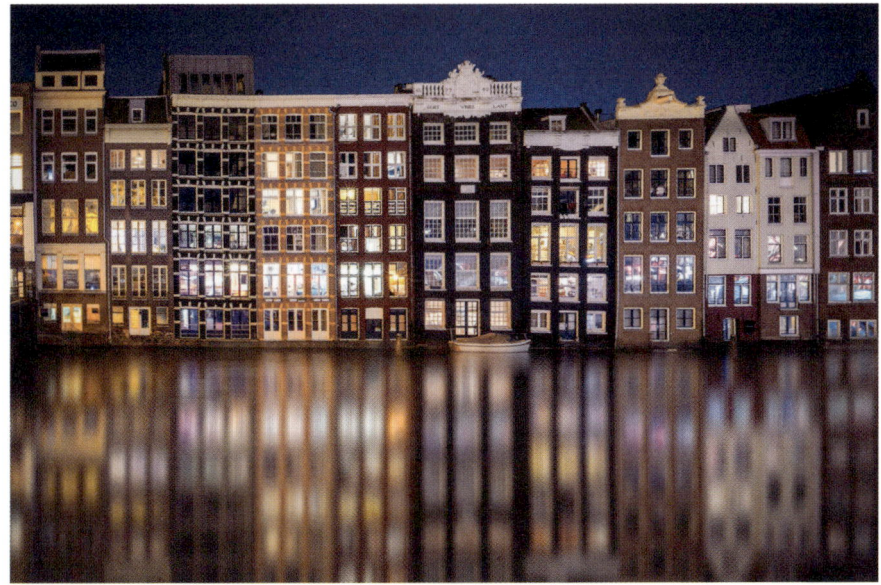

▲ *Although these traditional Dutch houses in Amsterdam were only partially reflected in the canals, the reflections add an extra dimension of interest and color to the overall scene.*

PRO TIPS

- Including a foreground element can create an additional layer of interest in your image.

- A camera with a tilting screen can help you shoot reflections in puddles from a low angle.

- Your reflections don't have to be precise mirrors—imperfect reflections can also be very effective.

TRAVEL NOTES

- Calm water is usually found early in the morning, but check the forecast to avoid windy days.

- Including a colorful sunset or sunrise in your reflections can add an extra layer of color and interest.

- Rainy weather can make a lot of surfaces reflective. At night, roads will reflect urban lights, adding color to your images.

- You can produce interesting abstract patterns and textures by focusing on colorful reflections and the different shapes they make.

ASSIGNMENT 02

_____

_____

_____

_____

_____

_____

_____

▶ *Taken at a tribal ceremony in Africa, this image doesn't need to reveal the full scene to tell the viewer what is going on. A tighter crop provokes more thought and requires the viewer to use his or her imagination to provide a fuller picture.*

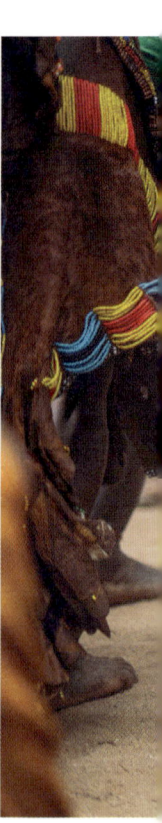

TECHNIQUE

There are various ways that you can emphasize the subject in your image:

- Zoom in to get closer.

- Use selective focus.

- Play with perspective and unusual shooting angles.

- Use light and shadow.

- Change the position of your subject in the frame.

- Control the background.

- Focus on shape, outline, or color.

- Accentuate one aspect of the subject.

SIGHTS UNSEEN

Intrigue and mystery are great ways to make a viewer stop and think about what is going on in your image. While some photographs are about documenting the immediate scene in front of you, sometimes *not* including everything can create a stronger and more powerful image. Leaving an element of mystery—part of a story that your viewer has to fill in—will help them engage with the photograph, as they try to understand what you were looking at.

For this assignment, the idea is to capture part of your subject so you only reveal a little bit about what is going on in the scene. You can decide if the parts you include reveal what or who your subject is, or whether you want to make it harder for your viewer to decipher. Either way, don't include your entire subject or make your shot too obvious—you want to reveal enough to tell part of the story, and allow your audience to decode the rest.

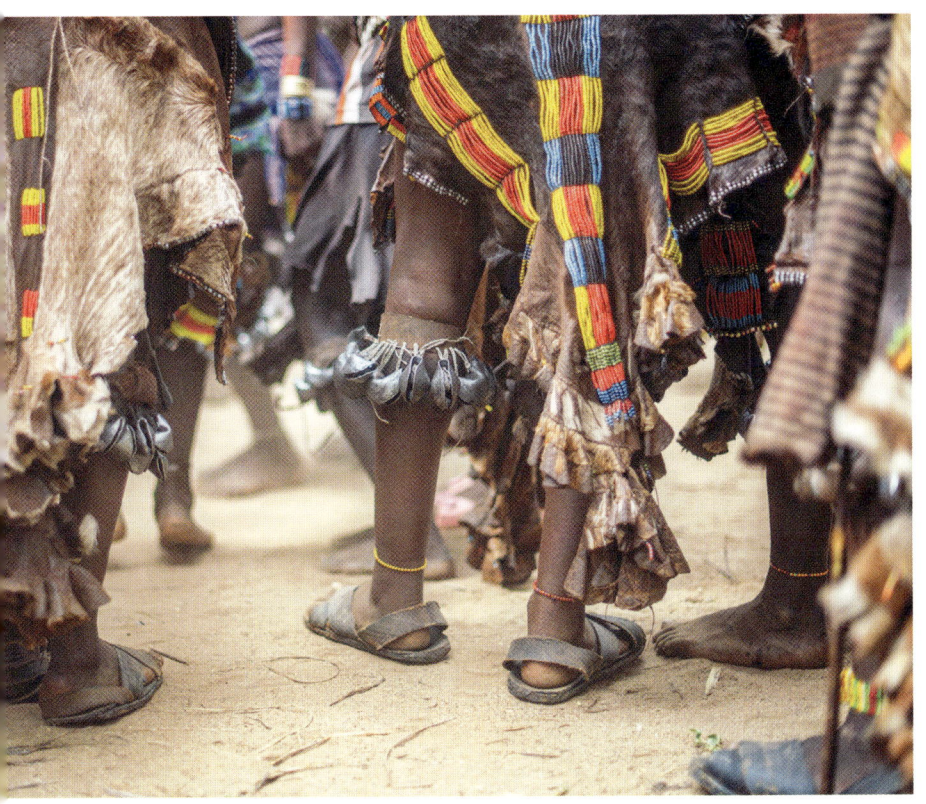

ASSIGNMENT

03

TECHNIQUE

- Start at the beginning. An initial scene-setting image will show your audience what is going on and/or the surroundings of your subject. Consider using a wideangle lens to reveal the environment to your audience.

- You may then want to zoom in on details to reveal a little bit more about the subject and their context.

- Try to use your final images to reveal the "ending" of the story.

TRAVELOGUE

Sometimes one image really won't do a scene justice. There may not be a single "definitive" shot and you will need to take a sequence of photographs to capture the essence of what is going on in front of you.

Your mission here is to tell a story about one particular aspect of your travel through a sequence of between six and eight images. It might be something special about your location, or you might want to reveal more about a particular subject or person. The idea is to use photography to help your audience understand what is going on and why. What are you telling them? Why are you deciding to share this? What is it that makes it so significant?

You are not creating a general travel article, but are aiming to capture a series of images that are all related to one another, so you have to be selective in what you include. Ensure that you don't include images that are unimportant or less relevant, as these will only end up in confusion. Each image should help tell part of the story and evoke a particular mood.

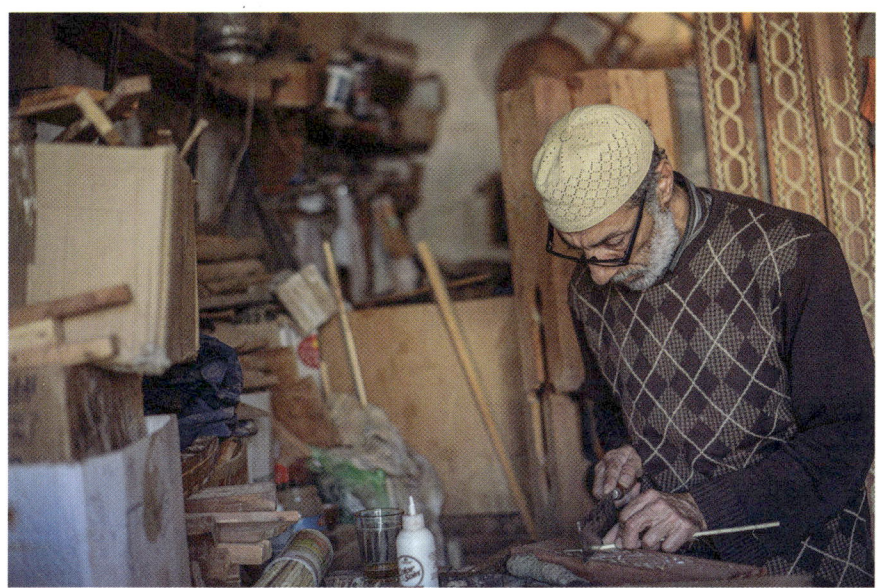

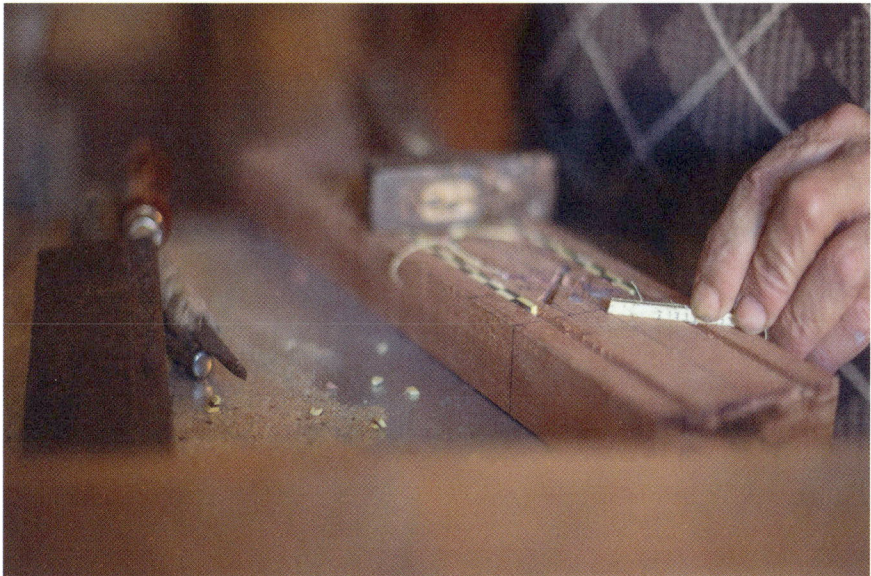

▲ ▶ The sequence of images above and on pages 14–15 shows a craftsman in Morocco working in his studio to create intricate wooden boxes. The first image sets the scene, the intermediate images focus on the details of this skilled work, and the final image reveals him proudly holding the finished product.

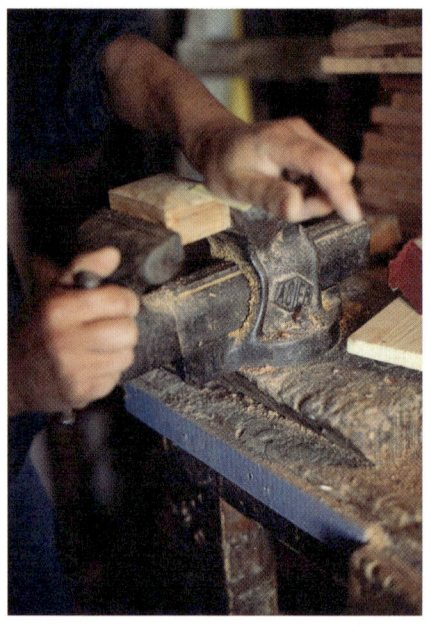

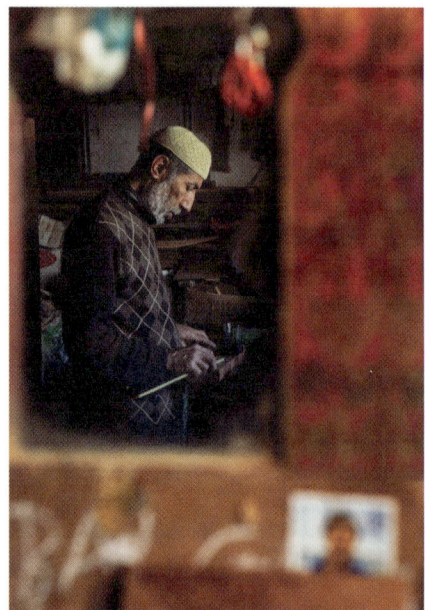

TRAVEL NOTES

You could use this assignment to help document different aspects of your trip, such as:

- A journey between places.

- A festival, celebration, or other ceremony.

- People you meet at a particular place.

- Animals you encounter on a safari.

- People at work or creating something, such as manufacturing or cooking.

- A visual exploration of a particular area or place.

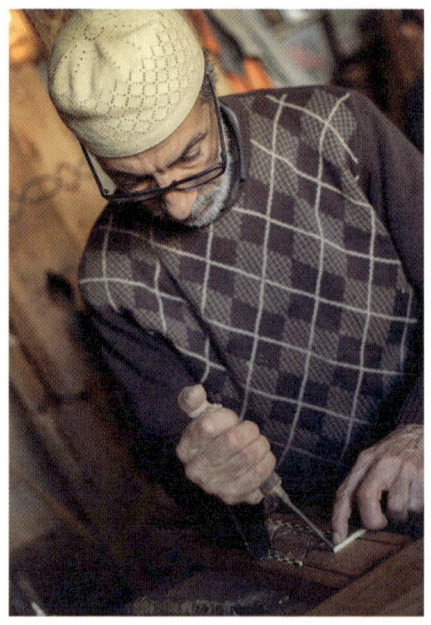

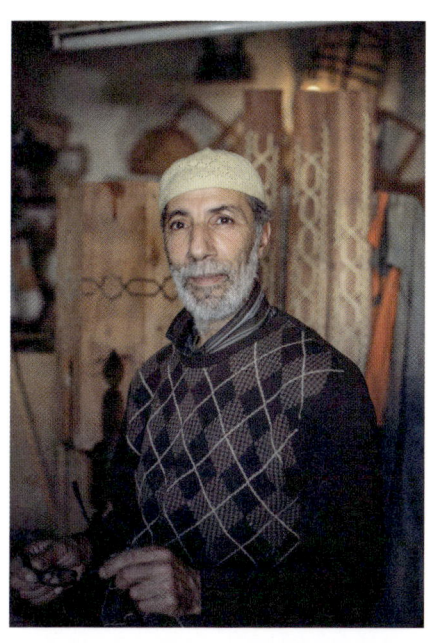

PRO TIPS

- Don't be afraid to mix horizontal and vertical shots. Sticking to one orientation can become repetitive.

- So your set hangs together well, it is best to stick to black and white or color, rather than mixing the two, so decide on your preferred treatment before you begin.

- Start by considering the first and last images, as this will help you decide on the key shots in between.

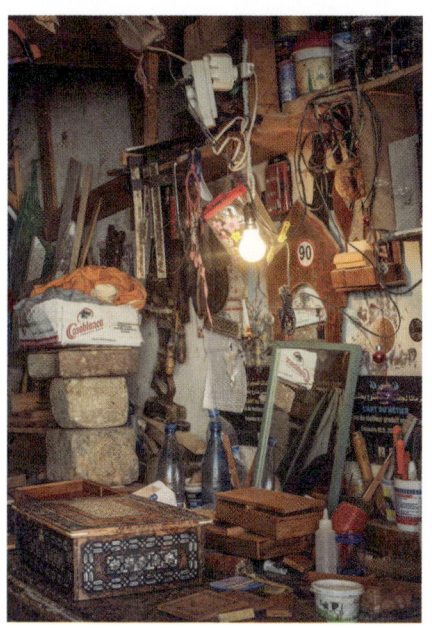

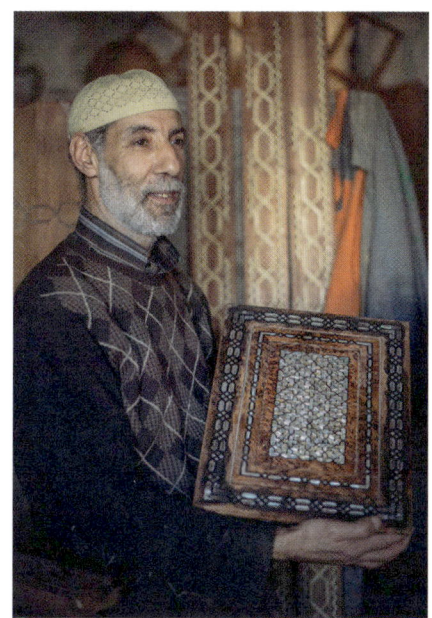

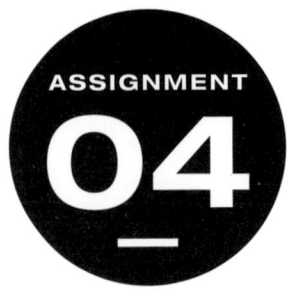

TECHNIQUE

- Lenses can be key to your composition. A wideangle lens will capture more of the structure or view, while a telephoto can help you focus in on specific details and can achieve a shallower depth of field.

- Different times of day offer different light, which may help accentuate certain parts of the scene.

▶ *For this image of the Eiffel Tower in Paris, I decided to focus on the internal structure, rather than taking an image of it in its entirety. By focusing on a detail, from a unique angle, I have taken a widely photographed iconic structure and tried to create something a little different. You do not always need a telephoto or zoom lens to capture detail—I used a wideangle lens, and framed and processed the image to create an almost unrecognizable detail of the iconic tower.*

ALTERNATIVE POSTCARD

Most urban trips will lead you toward the popular landmarks of the city you are visiting. Whether it's the Eiffel Tower, the Golden Gate Bridge, or the Golden Temple, iconic sites will draw in intimidating (and obscuring) crowds of tourists. Famous locations are on the list of "must see" and "must photograph" views, and also perceived as instant (and Instagrammable) symbols of their host cities.

Mesmerized by such sights, many photographers simply point their camera and snap away. However, for this assignment your brief is to ask yourself how you can achieve your own unique composition while still capturing the essence of the landmark. Your mission is to create an alternative to the common "postcard" view. Think about the thousands of people who visit the site on a daily basis and where they all stand to take thousands of the same image. Find your own special angle and create a photograph that is individual to you. This will not be an easy task! When your mission is complete, print your six most distinctive compositions as "alternative" postcards.

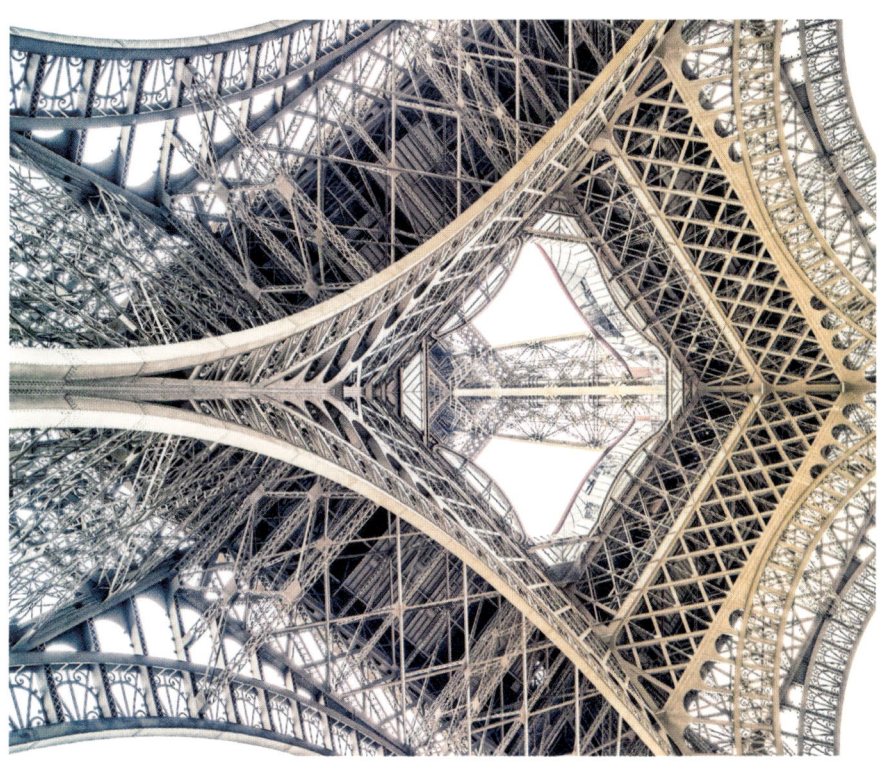

TRAVEL NOTES

- Plan ahead by looking online for an unusual vantage point or for an inspirational image of the location to see what works (or doesn't).

- Check opening times if appropriate and try to arrive before the crowds turn up or after they've gone home.

- Make use of apps to check the relevant sunrise, sunset, blue hour, golden hour, and moon stages, to find interesting light.

PRO TIPS

- Try to find a unique angle or position from which to shoot.

- Use sunlight to achieve strong highlights or shadows.

- Think outside the box and move away from where most other photographers are standing. If you find yourself alone then you are starting to meet the brief.

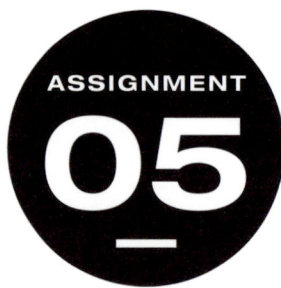

ASSIGNMENT 05

▼ *This natural rock arch on the Jurassic Coast in the UK is shown photographed at two different times here and on pages 20–1. This first shot was taken just as the sun dipped below the horizon, revealing the isolated cove and the grassland dotted with wild flowers.*

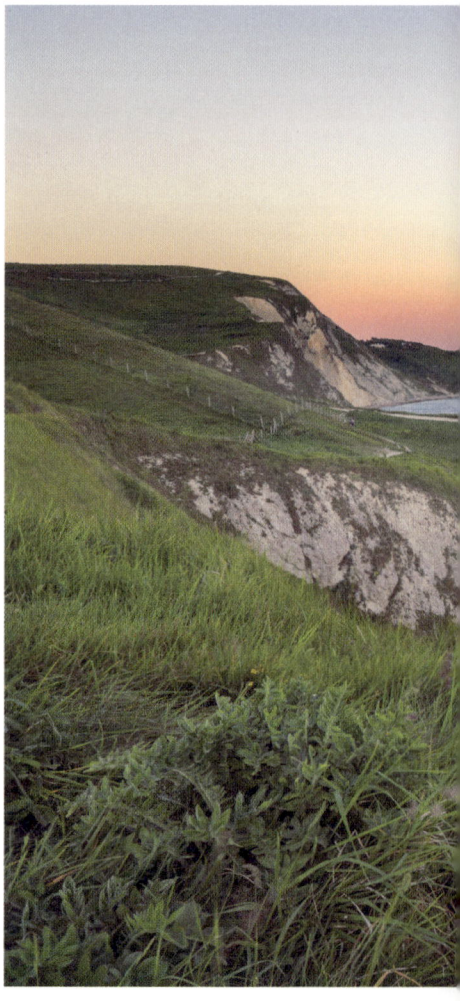

TECHNIQUE

- It can be difficult to anticipate how an area will change over a period of time, so there is a certain amount of trial and error in this assignment.

- Think about different times of day and how this affects the scene. When the sun is low on the horizon, or it's cloudy, you will have softer light than when it is high in the sky, for example.

- Look around the location for artificial lights, such as streetlights or the lights in nearby buildings, and consider how they might change the scene after dark.

THE IMAGE THAT NEVER SLEEPS

The decision to shoot during the day or to take your camera out at night can have a big impact on your images and the mood that you capture. A location can take on a completely different look depending on whether it is wrapped in bright sunlight or illuminated by artificial lights once the sunlight fades. Your brief for this assignment (continued on pages 20–1) is to return to the same place and capture a pair (or set) of images that reveals the changes in a scene at different times of the day and night. Scout ahead for a great location and think about the subject and scene. Start by carefully considering your composition and framing.

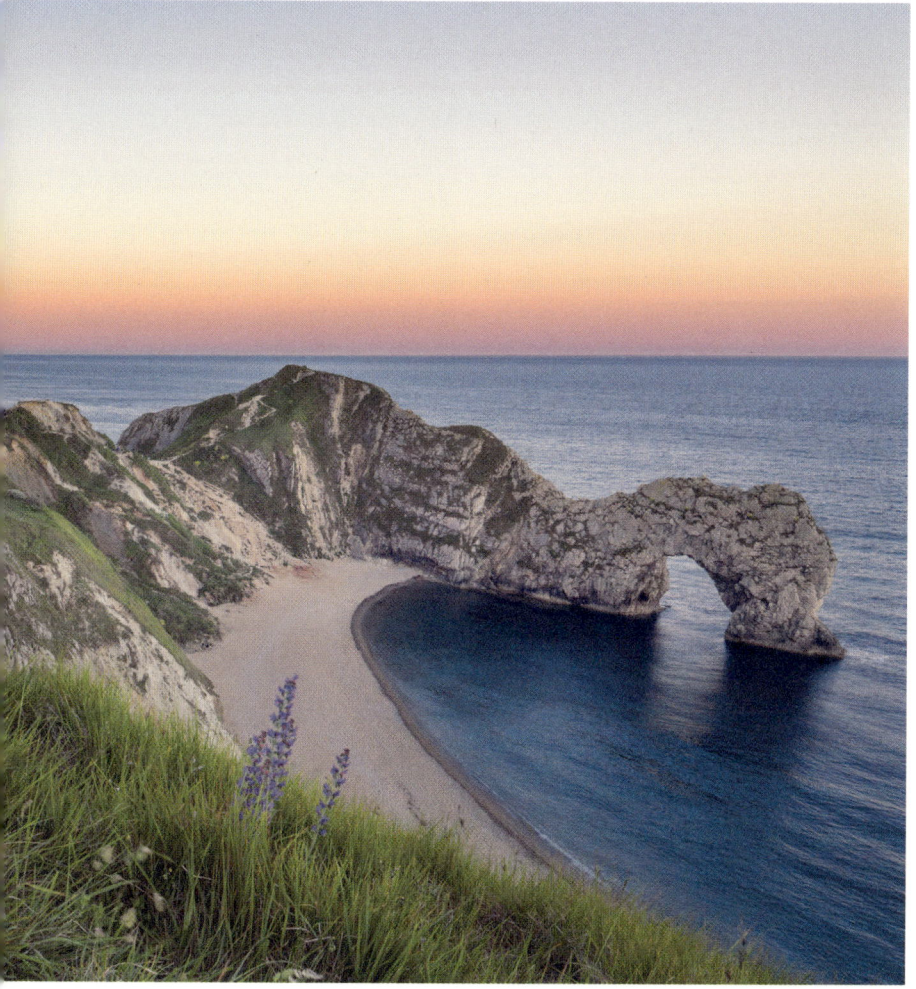

► *This photograph was taken a few hours after the shot on the previous page and reveals the wonder of the Milky Way rising behind the arch. There is a completely different feel to the image, even though it was taken from the same spot and is of the same subject.*

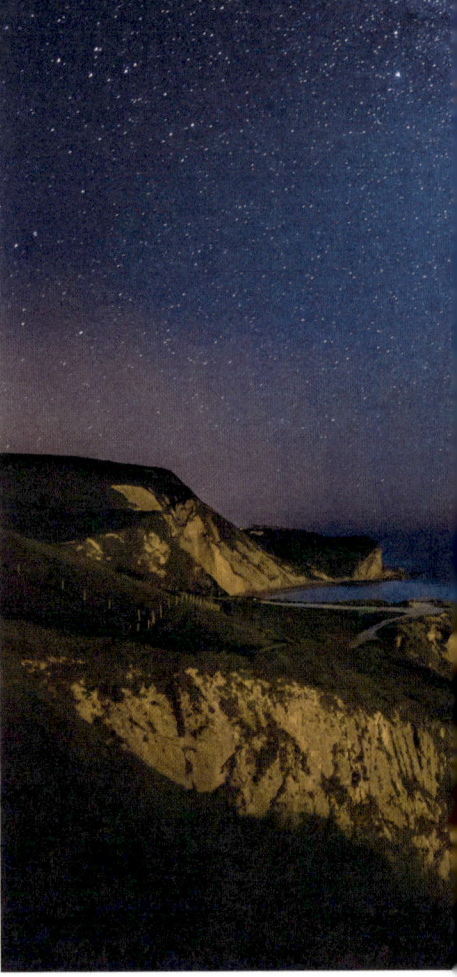

PRO TIPS

• Take care when photographing at night, especially when traveling in an area you do not know. Some places can become less safe after dark, whether you are in an urban environment or out in the wilderness.

• This type of photography is called "rephotography," which is the act of repeatedly photographing the same site at different times.

Develop your concept by trying to visualize how the area might change at different times of the day, and what aspects will potentially make it interesting to your viewer. Perhaps it is deep shadows created by harsh sunlight, the emptiness at night, or the artificial lights that mingle with twilight?

Your images don't have to be identical, but they should focus on the same area or subject. To complete your assignment, select and print a pair of images that capture your chosen travel location at two contrasting times. The results can be stunning.

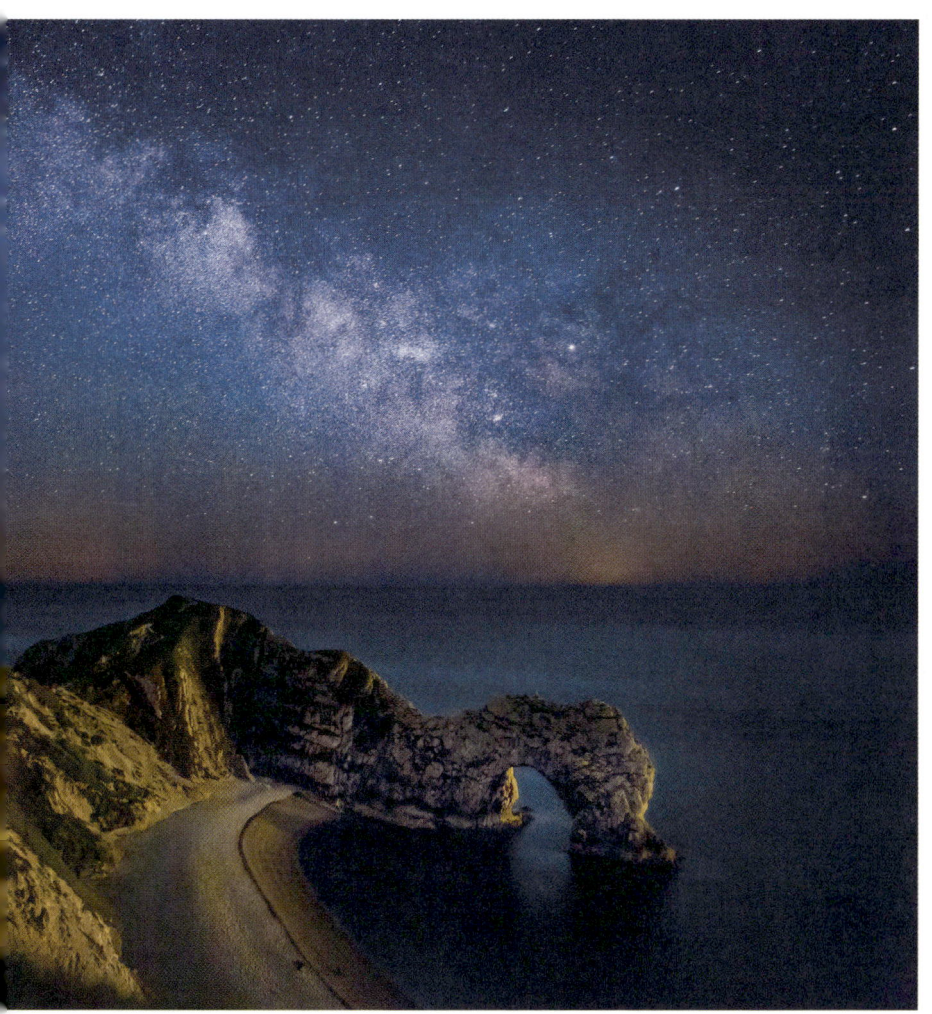

ASSIGNMENT JOURNAL

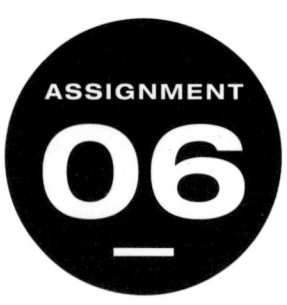

ASSIGNMENT 06

TECHNIQUE

- A flip-out screen on your camera will help you shoot from low angles and when you hold your camera up high.

- A wideangle lens will appear to accentuate the areas closest to the camera when you shoot from low down, emphasizing the foreground in your images.

- Look for compositional elements, such as leading lines—shooting from "unusual" angles will let you use them in a different and effective way.

- Consider using a zoom lens when shooting from up high to pick out details in a scene.

TRAVEL NOTES

- The internet has a wealth of information that will help you find unique views. Local maps and other resources can often suggest different vantage points.

- Holding your camera above your head can be effective if you are shooting in a crowd. You can also use a monopod or tripod to help you gain extra height.

- Walk around and explore your location. See what different and interesting viewpoints you come across as you go.

PRO TIPS

- Take a range of images from a variety of different positions so you can see which ones work best.

- Taking a few steps in a different direction will completely change your composition, so don't stand still for too long!

- A beanbag or mini-tripod can be useful if you don't want to put your camera directly on the ground.

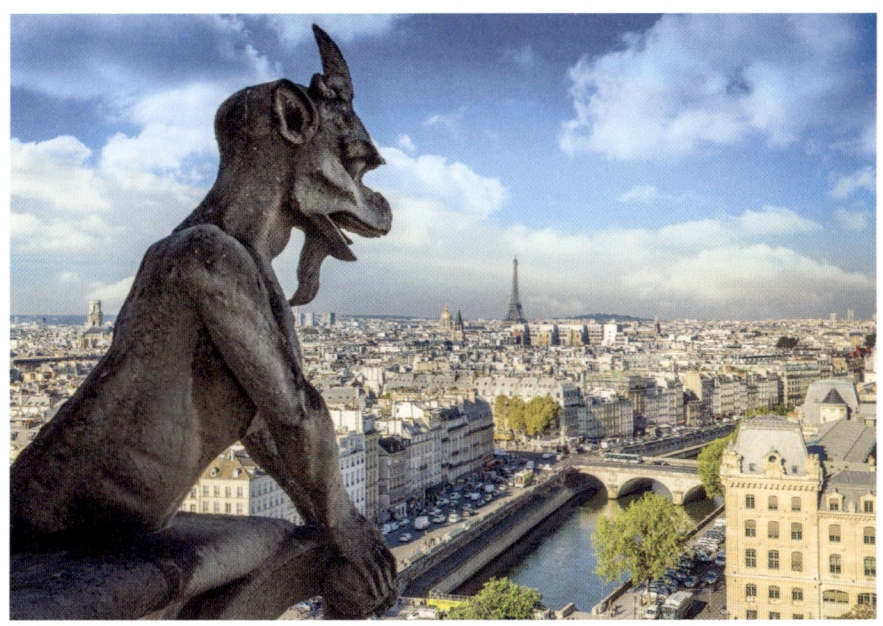

▲ *This stone gargoyle overlooks the city of Paris, France, from high up on Cathédrale Notre-Dame de Paris. It provides strong foreground interest while revealing some of the river and city streets below.*

ADMIRE THE VIEW

Eye-level is naturally the most common position for photographers to shoot from, but simply lifting the camera up to our eyes and taking a shot can result in an obvious and uninspiring image that will be familiar to anyone who has been to the same location. More exciting compositions—and therefore more memorable images—are often captured where the camera is placed somewhere different to the norm.

The assignment here is to get as creative as possible with your viewpoint. Get down really low, climb up high, twist or turn—do whatever it takes to change your perspective and produce photographs that aren't taken from eye-level.

Once you have decided what you want to photograph, think about how you can capture it from a more unique position. Do you need to walk around to find a higher vantage point or is there somewhere close by that gives you a different angle? Perhaps you just need to lie prone or squat down? Either way, you should be able to come up with a more unique image by changing the angle you shoot from.

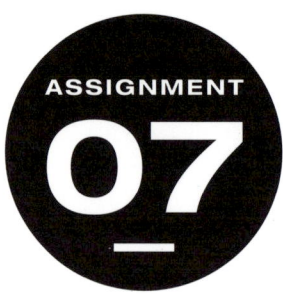

ASSIGNMENT

07

TECHNIQUE

- Make sure you focus on the eyes, as these are the "windows to the soul."

- Shooting portraits at eye-level makes your images more personal and less imposing. This will also ensure that you convey a connection with your subject.

- Play with the aperture to change the depth of field and determine how much of the background is in focus.

- Try to fill the frame with your subject so you really capture the details of their face.

- Using a focal length in the region of 50–100mm will result in natural-looking, undistorted images.

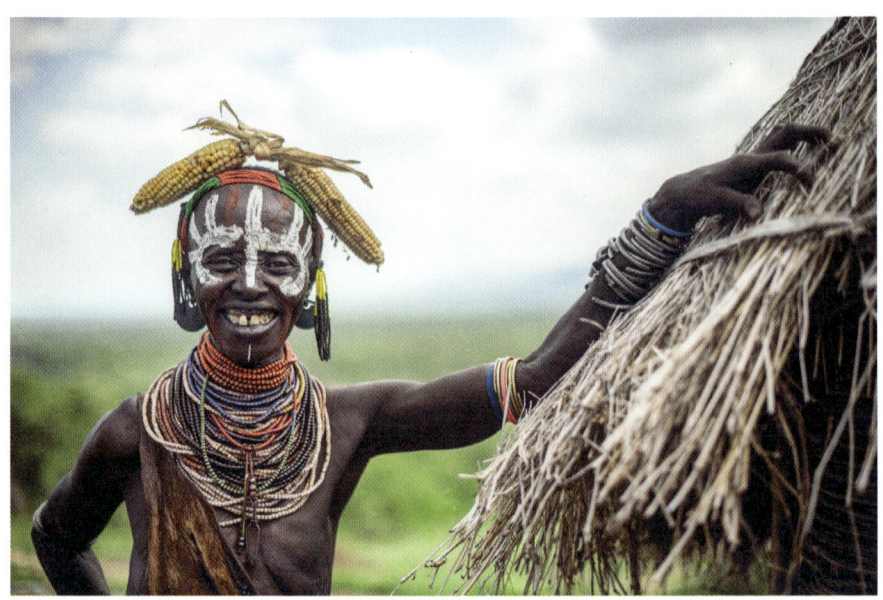

▲ *Although she didn't speak any English, a nod and a smile confirmed this woman from the Karo tribe on the banks of the Omo River in Ethiopia was happy to have her portrait taken.*

MEET THE LOCALS

Portraits of the people you meet on your travels are a popular subject and for good reason. Traveling around you will naturally encounter people from different cultures, often with unique dress, traditions, jobs, and other cultural traits. These differences can not only make for compelling and interesting travel portraits, but are also a great way of learning more about where you are and what it is like to live there.

Sometimes you will find yourself in a far-flung destination where you don't speak the same language as the locals, but your assignment here is to try to communicate a request to take someone's portrait. There are many ways that you can try to do this, including learning a few key phrases, smiling, and perhaps pointing to your camera. Always be courteous and respectful. Although you may find the experience a little intimidating at first, often you will be pleasantly surprised at people's willingness to be photographed. It can be a rewarding experience, and the route to a great portfolio of travel portraits.

TRAVEL NOTES

- Learn a few basic phrases in the native language such as "please," "thank you," "what is your name?"

- Make eye contact and see if it is returned. This is sometimes a clear way of finding out if your subject is not keen to have their photograph taken.

- Make sure you show your subject the image on the back of your camera—perhaps offer to send it to them by email or as a printed copy.

PRO TIPS

- Consider dialing in the relevant camera settings (such as aperture and ISO) before you ask, so you are ready to shoot and don't have to keep your subject waiting.

- It is easy to rush, but don't panic, as you'll likely end up with a bad image. Try to take things slowly, check your exposure, and ensure you have a nicely composed and well-focused image before you say goodbye.

ASSIGNMENT JOURNAL

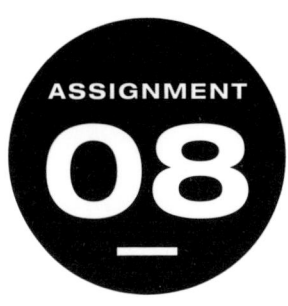

ASSIGNMENT
08

TECHNIQUE

- Using a macro or telephoto lens will make it easier to focus on individual elements and remove irrelevant distractions.

- Consider using a shallow depth of field to blur the background and concentrate attention on the subject.

- Changing lenses will help ensure that you have variety within your images.

▶ *Small details can create a sense of "place." This starfish—contrasting against the wooden texture of an old fishing hut—really stood out and was one of many that I saw as I explored a remote fishing village.*

DETAILS, DETAILS

Whether you are standing on top of a mountain in front of a sweeping vista, in a jungle, or looking down a narrow cobblestone alley in an ancient city, it is easy to be overwhelmed by the immediate view of everything you can see and to overlook the small details within. Yet it is often the small details that help tell the story of where you are. They may seem insignificant when compared to their surroundings, but it is the small elements that help to create the bigger picture.

Your assignment is to capture between five and eight images that hone in on the smaller features of your setting—features that evoke a sense of where you are and what you are seeing. Wander around slowly and look carefully, thinking about the individual elements and how they combine to give a sense of location. If you removed them from your current environment, how would that change your perception of a place?

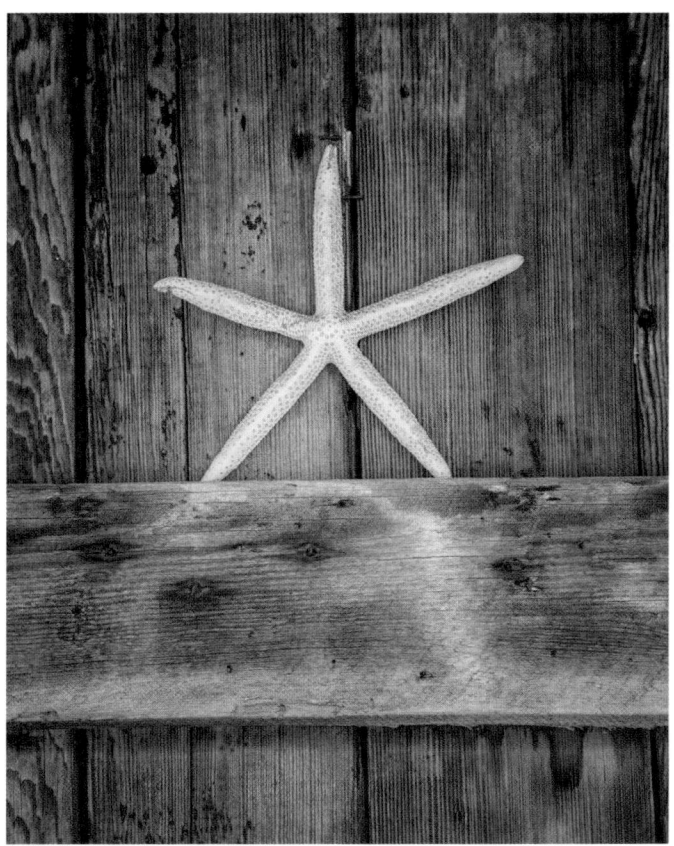

PRO TIPS

- Choose a subject or part of one that is strong enough to become the center of a simple yet powerful image.

- Details don't always have to be small—they can just be a smaller part of a large scene or vista.

- Play around with shape, color, texture, patterns, and lines, as these all make for interesting imagery.

- Use your image-editing program's cropping tool in postproduction to change the composition and experiment with different framing.

TRAVEL NOTES

- Think about what you are focusing on and how it relates to where you are. How does the detail reveal a sense of time and place?

- Try to include enough information in your composition to suggest an interesting and understandable story behind your subject. Your viewers should be able to tell why you chose to focus in on that particular element.

- Look around for small details that tell an intimate story, whether they are natural or man-made.

ASSIGNMENT 09

TECHNIQUE

- There is no right way to make an abstract image, but simplicity is often a key to success. Try not to clutter your image with too many competing ideas.

- Don't make your subject too easily recognizable. You want to challenge your viewer to come to his or her own conclusion about what it is.

- Lighting can play an important role and can be used to emphasize key elements in the frame.

- Composition is crucial, so think about what to include and what to leave out.

- Playing with your angle of view can help add a sense of mystery and alter obvious shape and form.

- Changing the colors of a scene, either in-camera with the white balance setting or during postproduction, can create interesting results.

PRO TIPS

Some themes to focus on might be:

- Color
- Texture
- Light and dark
- Shadows and highlights
- Patterns, lines, and repetition
- Movement and blur
- Shape and design
- Angles
- Reflections and other distortions
- Negative space
- Contrast
- Mystery, mood, and emotion

ASSIGNMENT JOURNAL

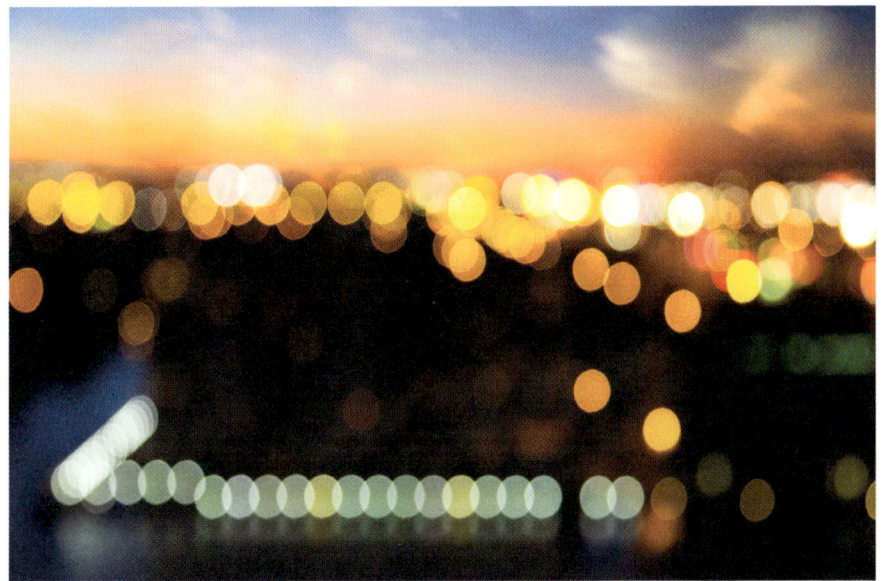

▶ *The shimmering city lights in the distance seem to sit magically with the wonderful sunset colors in the sky. Rather than capture this scene accurately, I chose to make a more abstract image. Using a wide aperture of f/1.8 and slightly defocusing produced a dreamy effect.*

IMAGINARY JOURNEY

So you have finally made it—all that time and effort to make it to a new and wonderful destination has paid off! But before you start trying to capture all of the breathtaking sights in front of you, let's explore a different technique.

Abstract photography is a broad term, but generally refers to an image that is undefined and ambiguous—one where your viewer will not immediately be certain about what the subject is. So, instead of trying to capture a beautifully accurate representation of what you can see, think about ways to make a more elusive and imprecise photograph. The idea here is to create an image that makes your viewer question what it is they are seeing and where it may be. It should provoke their imagination, and stimulate thought and emotion, rather than focusing on the obvious.

This sounds complicated, but in fact it is quite the opposite (although not easy to do well). There is an infinite number of potential abstract photographs all around you as you read this. Look and think about the individual elements that make up your current location. Consider how you can utilize what is around you to create simple yet elegant and uncomplicated images.

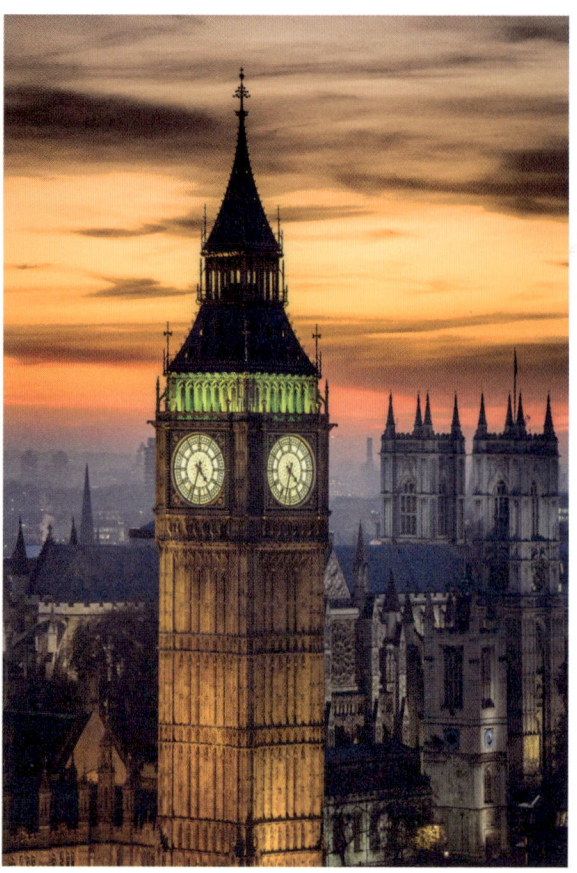

▲ *The iconic Elizabeth Tower—home to Big Ben in London—was standing proud during a spectacularly colorful sunset. While many photographers pack up and leave once the sun has gone down, it pays to hang around a little longer, as this is often when the colors really light up the sky.*

TECHNIQUE

- You will usually need to use longer shutter speeds during the "golden hour," so watch out for camera shake. Increasing your ISO can often help.

- The light changes quickly at these times of day, so keep an eye on your exposure.

- Your white balance setting can help accentuate the warm colors of the sunlight. The Cloudy or Shade settings will add warmth to an image.

- Placing the sun behind your subject can give a magical backlit glow.

SUNSEEKER

Quite often we associate travel with sun and sunshine, but this isn't always the case. However, no matter where you are, the first and last light of the day can be really special. Photographers have given these times a name, with the period shortly after sunrise and just before sunset known as the "golden hour."

With the sun low on the horizon, the sunlight is soft and directional, casting long shadows that provide depth to your images. This warm color of the light is also associated with calm and happiness.

Your assignment is simple: get up early or stay out until the sun starts to set and capture something—anywhere or anyone—bathed in the magical golden light of sunrise or sunset. Make the most of your subject or view as it is enveloped by the soft, warm, yellow and orange tones, and the long shadows that can make your photographs seem more three-dimensional.

One of the other benefits of being out and photographing at these times—especially at sunrise—is the stillness and peace you can usually enjoy. Early in the morning a lot of people will still be in bed, so you can often avoid crowds and enjoy having your location almost to yourself.

TRAVEL NOTES

- Despite its name, the "golden hour" doesn't usually last for one hour. It lasts longer the further north or south of the equator you are, and is also affected by the time of year.

- There are plenty of apps that can tell you where and when the sun will rise and set for your specific location.

- Getting up early can help reveal what day-to-day life is like where you are, whether it's locals starting their day, wildlife unaffected by human presence, or simply a deserted beach without any footprints in the sand.

PRO TIPS

- A few clouds in the sky can help create a stunning sunrise or sunset.

- Arrive well before sunrise so you are in place and ready for the changing light.

- It is not only landscapes that will benefit from the light at these times of day. You can also create stunning portraits, while architecture can look great under soft, warm light as well.

- Don't forget to look all around you, as there is often wonderful light in all directions, not just in the direction of the rising or setting sun.

ASSIGNMENT

11

TECHNIQUE

- You will need to use a slow shutter speed to capture movement, which usually means your camera needs to be on a tripod, so the background remains sharp. Only the moving parts of the scene should be blurred.

- Panning is a slightly different form of blur, where you focus on a particular moving element, such as a car or train, and track it as you take a shot. Your subject will remain in relatively sharp focus, while the background is blurred.

LIFE IN MOTION

Almost everywhere you go, when you stop and look you will see that the world immediately around you is constantly moving. The speeds may be different, but whether it's nature, people, or the urban environment, things are rarely at a standstill. Your brief is to capture some element of this movement, and with it, the essence of your location. Experiment with motion and blur to communicate a feeling of what it is like to be in your chosen location, to show a sense of the pace of the place, and to reveal what happens slightly beyond the immediate moment you press the shutter-release button.

Too much movement will result in an abstract image (see Assignment 09), which can be harder for your viewers to understand and interpret, so you need to find the balance between creating a sense of motion and a feeling of the energy in your location, and reducing everything to a blur. The idea is not to be too conceptual, but to reinforce the sense of speed, movement, and action.

ASSIGNMENT JOURNAL

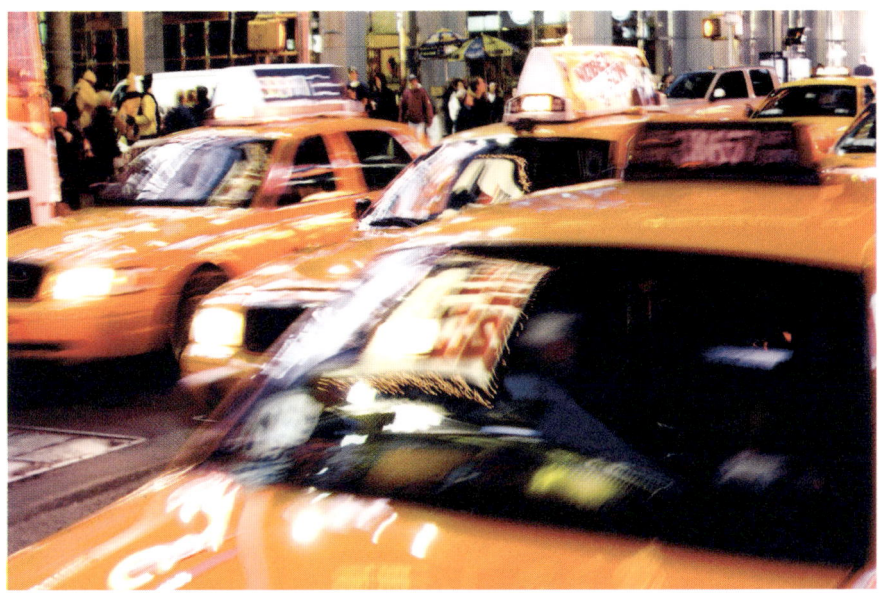

▲ *Times Square in New York City is a famously busy area in midtown Manhattan. To help accentuate how lively and congested the area is, I decided to capture the image with a slight blur. I used a slow shutter speed and gently moved the camera to add a little movement to the traffic, taking care not to overexpose the image.*

PRO TIPS

- A neutral density (ND) filter can help you extend the shutter speed by restricting the amount of light that enters the lens.

- A polarizing filter can also help to increase the exposure time by up to 2–3 stops.

TRAVEL NOTES

- Play with capturing movement in nature. Water generally looks interesting when it is blurred, and waterfalls make great subjects, with the blurred water giving them a dreamy feel.

- On a windy day you may find that moving trees, long grass, or sand blowing across a beach can add interest to your images.

- People and traffic are great subjects for this assignment, which will emphasize the hustle and bustle of urban life.

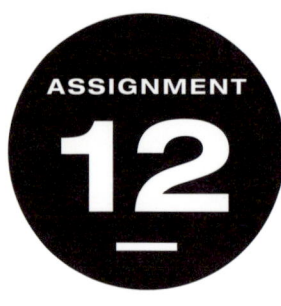

ASSIGNMENT

12

TECHNIQUE

- A cloudy day may result in more delicate, understated tones, creating a softer ambience for your photograph.

- Every color will bring a different feeling to your image: brighter colors can show energy or happiness; blues convey peace and calm; greens are associated with the natural world.

▼ *These beachside huts catch the eye thanks to the array of vibrant colors that disappear into the distance. The sunshine helps to accentuate the vibrancy of the colors, but keep in mind how the light might affect the colors when you are considering your final composition.*

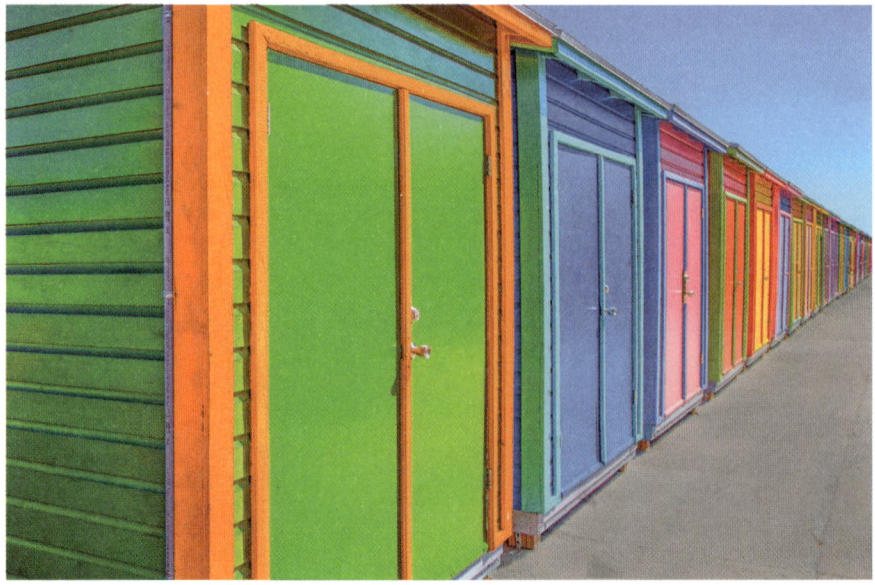

A SPLASH OF COLOR

We see the world in color, and color appears naturally everywhere we look, influencing our perception of where we are. There are warm colors, such as the yellow and orange hues associated with the sun; cooler blue tones; and of course, many more in between. All of these different colors affect our emotions and how we interpret what we are seeing.

For this assignment, set out to play with color in your photographs. You might try using strong, bold colors to place emphasis on one part of your image, and explore how color can draw your viewer's attention to different parts of the photograph. For example, where you have a multitude of similar colors and one area in a distinctly different color, note how that area immediately stands out.

Alternatively, you could photograph muted pastels to emphasize the overall color palette of a scene. Whichever route you take, your brief is to make color the hero of your travel assignment, so remember to frame your image to place the emphasis where you want it.

TRAVEL NOTES

- Think about how color relates to your location. You might choose to focus on one or two specific colors, perhaps relating to the flag of the country you are visiting.

- A cold winter trip might be shot with a palette of cooler tones, while a warmer climate could rely on the reds, yellows, and oranges of the sunshine.

- The more you look around you, the more you will see a common color base on which to focus your attention.

PRO TIPS

- Take care not to overwhelm your image with a barrage of competing colors.

- Look for bold colors that accentuate the shape and form of your subject.

- Explore subtle, soft tones that help your viewer to focus on the details in an image.

ASSIGNMENT

13

TECHNIQUE

- Take time to look around and be creative with your compositions.

- Think about the style of images you want to achieve.

- Consistency is important, as you want the set to work well together.

- Try not to mix color and black-and-white images for this assignment.

THEMES

When you arrive somewhere new, you can sometimes be overwhelmed by all the different sights and smells that greet you. It can be a little daunting to know what to photograph and there can be a temptation to start snapping away at everything. However, if you take time to look around your new surroundings you will often encounter a lot of similar elements.

Your assignment here is to create a set of photographs that are related in some way. The idea is to choose one particular common subject and to create a set of images based on this theme. Start by thinking about what you want your theme to be. You may find that it becomes immediately obvious, as there is something that is commonplace where you are, or you may have to look harder to connect the elements you see around you.

Don't just shoot anything and everything that fits into your theme, though—remain selective and consider how your images will work together as a set. Your subjects don't have to be identical, either, as strong variations on a common theme can often work extremely well.

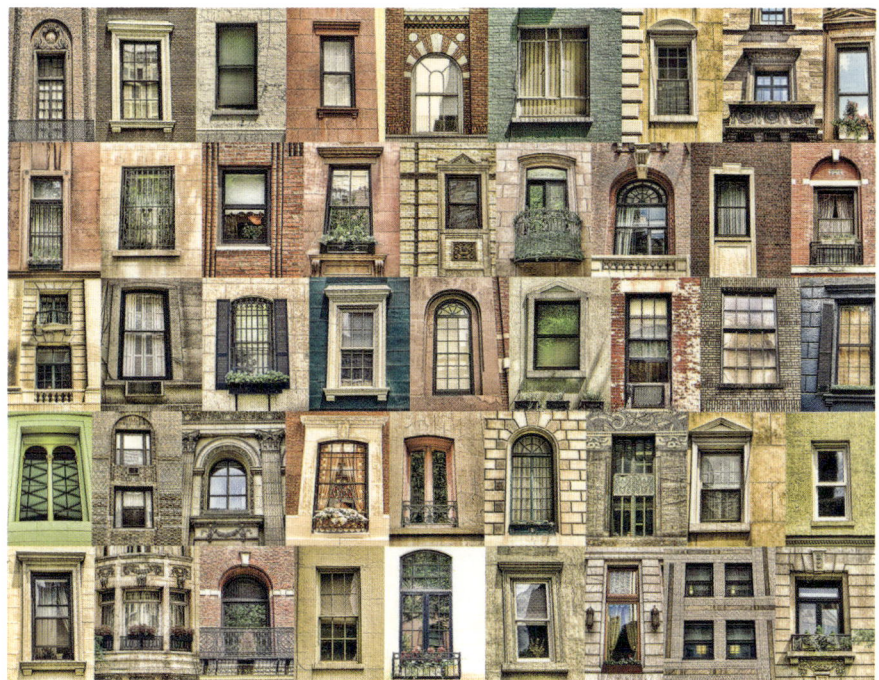

▲ *This image consists of a collection of windows that I photographed as I wandered through a city. I decided to photograph all of the interesting windows I passed and soon found I had a nice assortment of shots that I combined into a single image during postproduction.*

PRO TIPS

- Think about whether you want to create a set of images from a specific part of a trip, or whether you want them to represent your whole journey.

- Consider printing your images as a set, or creating a montage or larger composite in postproduction.

TRAVEL NOTES

- Some themes can help you tell the story of your travels, revealing a real sense of place based on what you regularly see.

- You could choose a physical theme, such as abandoned buildings, bicycles, street signs, or vintage cars.

- Flora and fauna can make interesting themes and will give your viewers real insight into the nature that is unique to the area you are visiting.

- Abstract concepts can also provide a great theme. Perhaps you could focus on a particular shape or feeling that you want your images to evoke?

ASSIGNMENT

14

TECHNIQUE

- Try to tell a story with your images, rather than simply showing various modes of transport in your location.

- Explore interesting angles and compositions, and include the wider environment to reveal more about the chosen means of transport.

- Think about your shutter speed and how you want to capture motion. You may want to use a slower shutter speed to record movement or light trails at night, or a fast shutter speed to freeze motion.

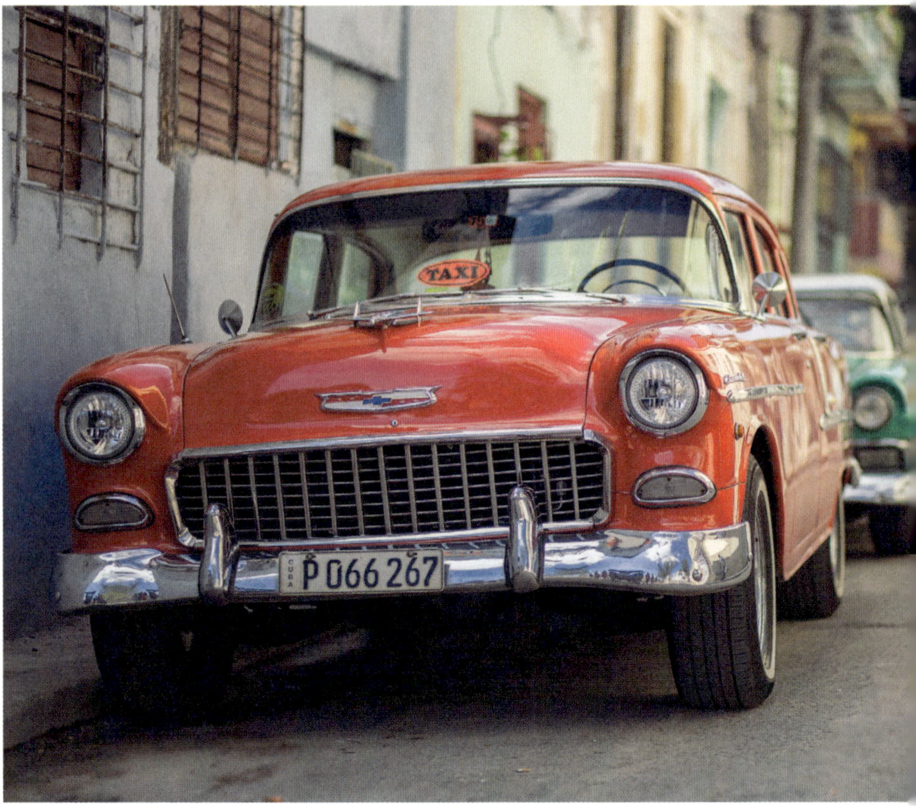

TRANSPORT OF DELIGHT

When you are heading off on your travels you will have to take some mode of transport to get to where you're going. Although this can sometimes be a tiring part of the journey, it can also be full of adventure and excitement. Your assignment (continued on pages 40–1) is to focus on the transport you see and use during your travels. Perhaps you have to take a seaplane to a distant island, for example, or you choose to take a rickshaw to whizz through urban streets, or you jump on a boat to cross a river?

You could also choose to focus on public transport, and the various options available to you or shared with local people. You could photograph passengers and transport workers, or maybe concentrate on places where people congregate to take or find transport, such as bus, subway, and railway stations, or taxi lines and truck stops. This should provide you with a wealth of opportunities for exceptional photographs.

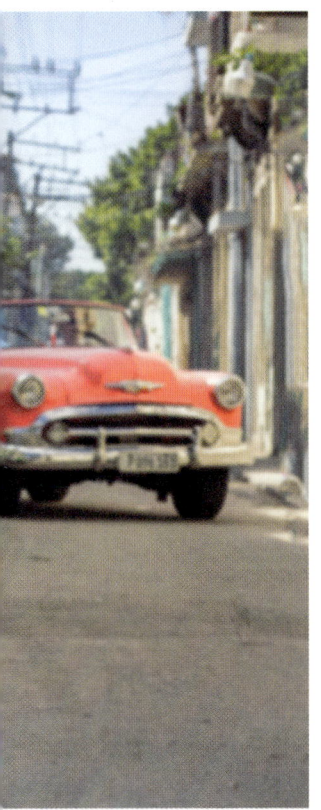

PRO TIPS

- Don't forget to capture some of the details that make the vehicles unique.

- Don't just capture the outside of a vehicle—the inside can often reveal a lot about your chosen subject.

- Transportation includes the movement of goods, not just people. Including this type of transport will add an additional layer of interest.

- This subject could make an interesting mini-project (see Assignment 03).

◄ *The iconic classic cars of Cuba make fantastic images and evoke a real sense of the country's history.*

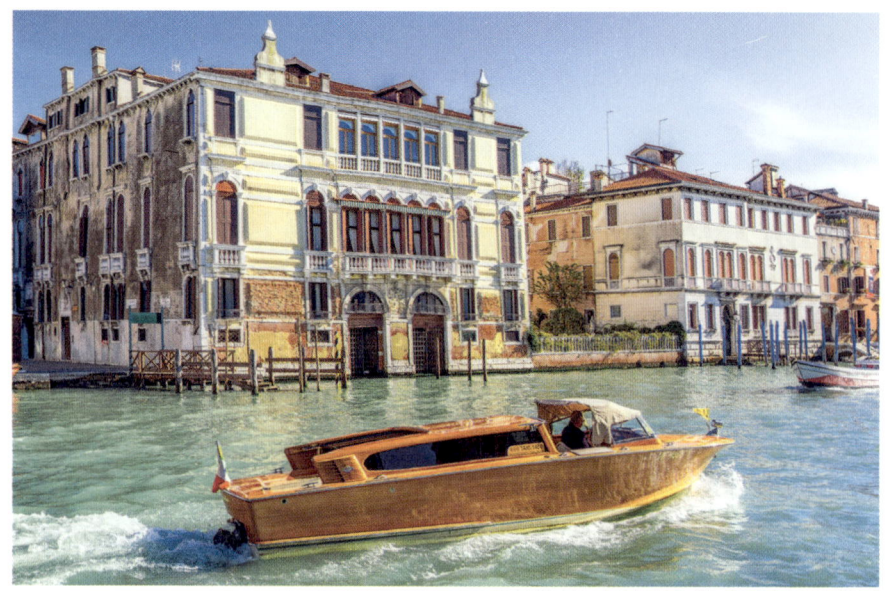

▲ *Venice in Italy is a unique city and the multitude of boats and gondolas on the water make great subjects for this assignment.*

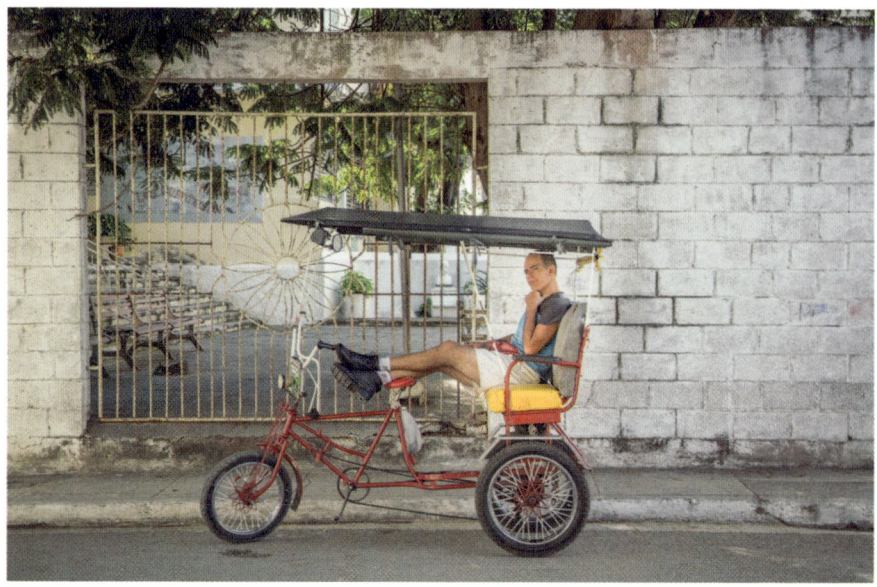

▲ *The people who operate public transport can also make strong images. Here, a rickshaw driver rests as he waits for a new fare.*

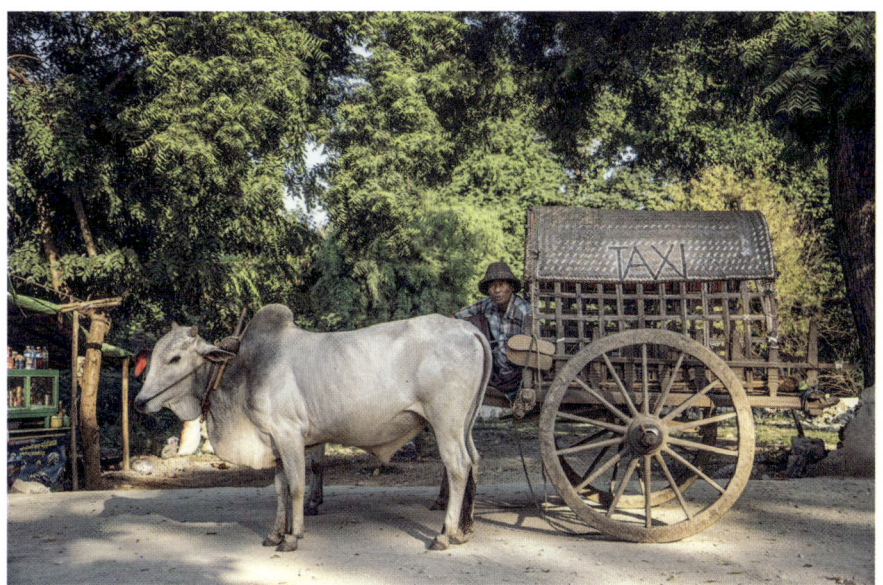

▲ *Transportation covers a wide range of subjects, such as this bullock-drawn taxi waiting for passengers in Southeast Asia.*

TRAVEL NOTES

- Ensure that you are not photographing in any forbidden areas. What may be fine to photograph at home may well be prohibited elsewhere.

- If you're going to capture the personality of the driver ensure that you don't distract him or her while taking photographs.

- Signs related to transportation can also help capture the essence of the place you're visiting, such as destination signs on the front of buses or at railway stations.

ASSIGNMENT JOURNAL

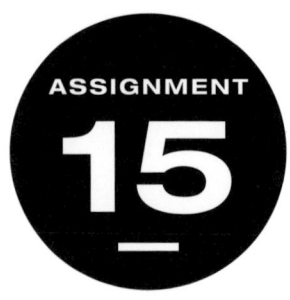

ASSIGNMENT 15

TECHNIQUE

- Think about your choice of lens and how this will affect your ability to photograph your subject.

- Consider preselecting the shutter speed so you are ready to freeze or blur motion.

- Auto ISO can help ensure that you obtain your preferred shutter speed.

- Always have your camera switched on so you are ready to take an image and won't miss any fleeting moments.

▶ *A cafe can be a great location to take refuge from a sudden downpour and can often provide you with a great viewpoint of the street life around you.*

CAFE SOCIETY

One of the small pleasures of traveling overseas is taking time to stop, sit back, and relax, and what better way to take a well-deserved rest than sitting in an outdoor cafe watching day-to-day scenes unfold in front of you?

But just because you're sitting down, that doesn't mean you have to put your camera away. Your assignment here is to watch what is happening around you and capture the essence of your location with a selection of images. You might decide to focus on passing traffic or people, or maybe the details of your immediate surroundings: what is it that makes where you are and what you see interesting?

The key here is not to rush and take all your images immediately, but to relax, wait, and observe. Be ready to photograph anything and everything of interest as it passes you by, rather than setting out and moving around to find your subjects.

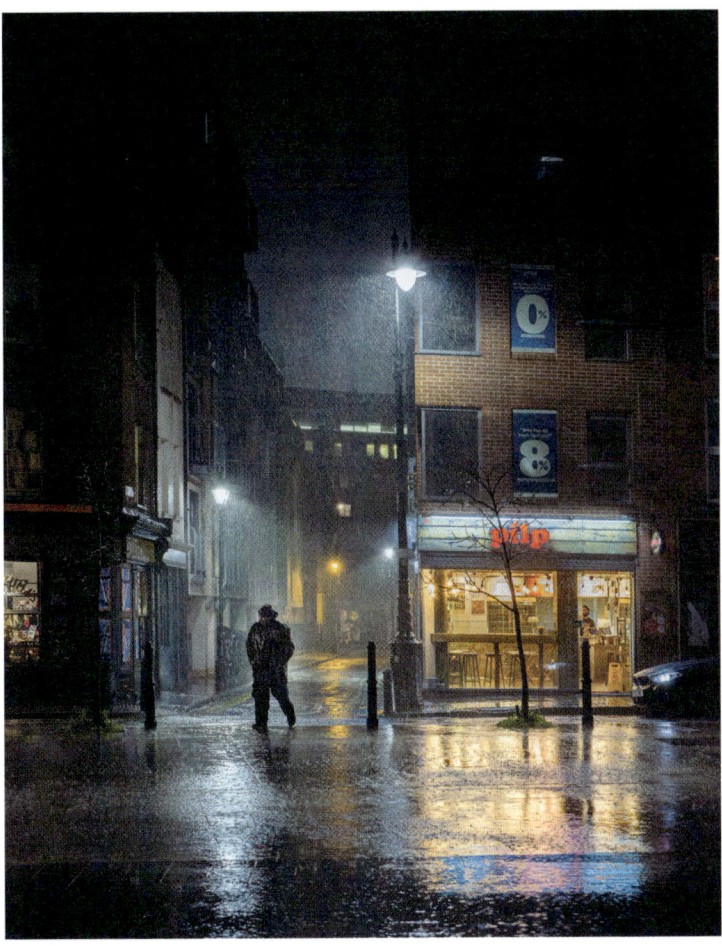

PRO TIPS

- Sometimes being stealthy and taking an image without holding the camera up to your eye can lead to some very creative and candid images.

- Don't forget to use windows, mirrors, and reflections in your shots.

- Be respectful and don't persist in taking someone's photograph if they clearly don't want you to.

TRAVEL NOTES

- Find a well-situated location, such as a coffee shop, bar, or restaurant.

- Look around for unique or individual elements that help tell the story about where you are.

- Be prepared for interesting moments to occur at any time.

ASSIGNMENT

16

TECHNIQUE

- Shoot before you sample! A freshly served dish will make a better photograph than one you have already tasted.

- Explore different angles. You may find that you have to take a few shots from different positions before you find the best light.

- Composition is really important for food photography, so decide if you want to include your surroundings or would prefer your shot to be more minimal.

- Overhead angles can provide interesting images, but make sure you fill the frame.

TRAVEL NOTES

- Don't just think about restaurants. You can also consider street food vendors, markets, and stalls, or even food served in a homestay.

- Take a cookery lesson and capture your own creative culinary delights.

- Does the presentation or background tell you anything about the culture or how the food is traditionally served?

- Great photographs can be found in the preparation of food, so don't forget to search out chefs and open kitchens.

- Think about asking locals for tips on where to eat and get a great local food experience.

- Be aware of local food-related customs. In Japan, for example, you shouldn't place your chopsticks vertically into a bowl, while in Thailand a fork is used only to place food onto a spoon to eat with.

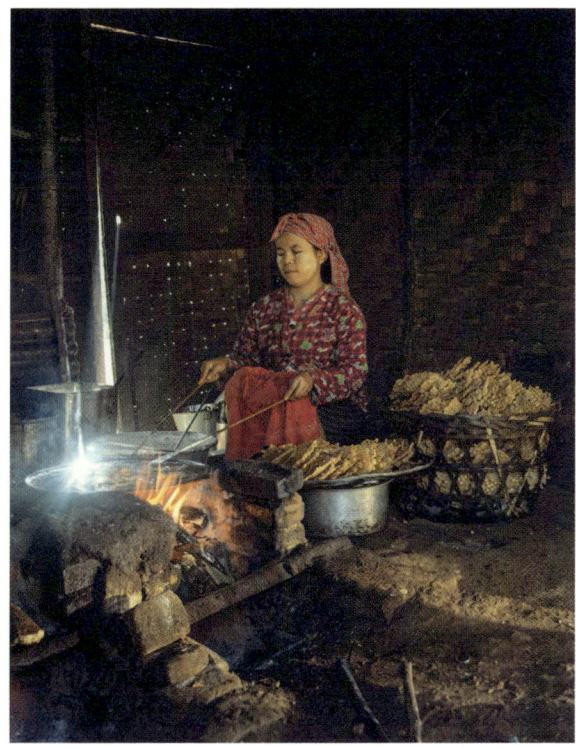

◄ *This image of a woman in Myanmar frying a popular local snack over an open fire captures the essence of her makeshift "kitchen."*

EAT LIKE A LOCAL

Sampling fresh local food is something we all look forward to, and most travel photography should include food—it is a big part of telling the story about the culture and location you are visiting.

Almost all countries, regions, and even villages will have specialty dishes that are unique to that place, but don't just focus on the final plate that is served to you. Capturing all aspects relating to food will help create a strong set of images that relate to a particular place and its cuisine. This can range from buying and selling food, to preparing, serving, and tasting it.

This assignment will be a little tricky, as it can be difficult to photograph food well. In certain places it will be almost impossible to control how it is served or the lighting—there certainly won't be any food stylists or professional lighting equipment! But you should still be able to come away with some great food images. Yes, it can be challenging, but that makes it more fun and rewarding. And, of course, there is the added bonus that you get to enjoy tasting the local cuisine as well!

ASSIGNMENT
17

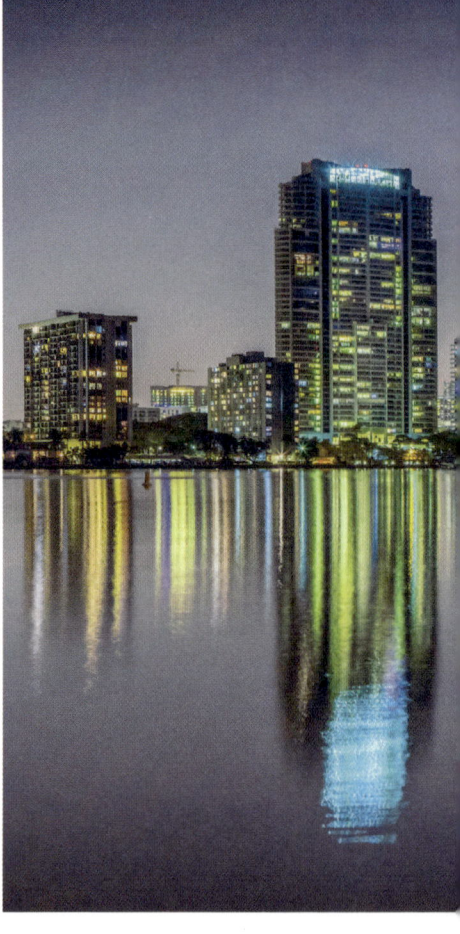

▲ *I located this spot overlooking downtown Miami during the day and knew that I would return once the sun had set to take this image. The strength of the building's lights reflected in the water adds an extra dimension and helps create a stronger and more dynamic cityscape.*

TECHNIQUE

- Try to take your images before the sky gets too dark. The "blue hour" is the period shortly after sunset and is the best time to shoot.

- You will need to keep your camera stable, as long shutter speeds will be needed. A tripod and remote release will help give the best results.

- Use manual focus, as your camera's autofocus will struggle in low light. Your camera's Live View mode can help you to focus accurately.

- Shoot Raw format images so you capture more data to edit in postproduction.

- You can create a starburst effect with point light sources such as streetlights by setting a small aperture in the region of f/16–f/22.

- It is easy to overexpose the highlights due to the intensity of artificial lights, so keep an eye on your camera's histogram.

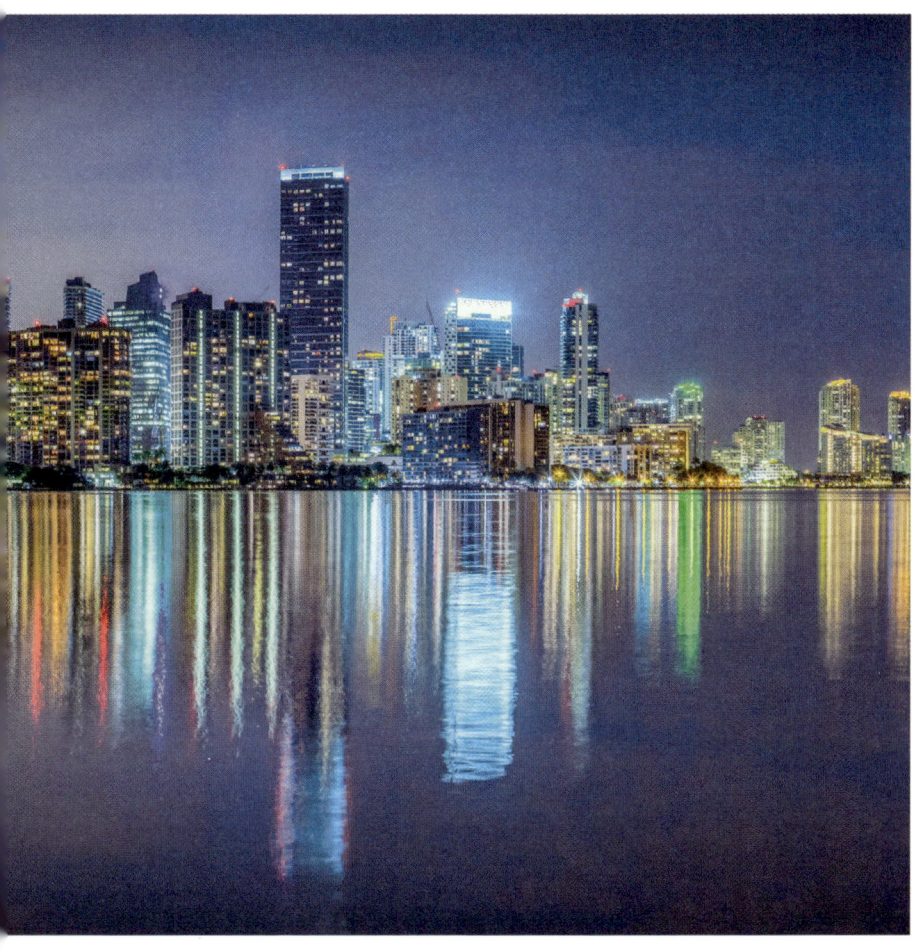

BRIGHT LIGHTS, BIG CITY

There is definitely something magical that happens when the sun goes down, as the sky turns an inky blue and the city (literally) starts to buzz with electricity. Urban areas really come alive when the sun sets, so when the lights come on and start to illuminate streets and buildings, head out with your camera, rather than packing up for the night.

Your brief (continued on pages 48–9) is to set out as the sun is starting to go down, with the aim of creating five dynamic urban images, including a full cityscape. Wait for a nice balance between the city lights and the early evening sky, and you will be able to create some fantastic and energetic images. For your wider cityscape, it will help to have a viewpoint in mind, so you are not just wandering around without direction.

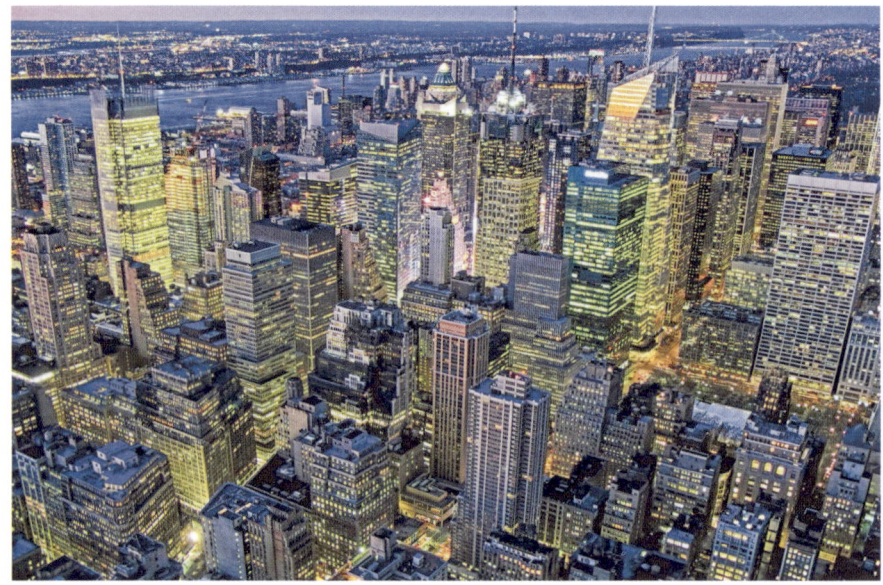

▲ Manhattan has numerous tall buildings and some have viewing decks that are open to the public. Online research can help find these and give you information such as opening hours, cost, and whether you can use a tripod.

PRO TIPS

- Long shutter speeds will turn moving traffic into streaks of light as it passes through the frame.

- Your camera's Bulb mode will enable you to use shutter speeds longer than 30 sec. Use a remote release to hold open the shutter for as long as you want.

- A "fast" lens (one with a maximum aperture of f/2.8 or wider) will let more light reach the camera's sensor and reduce exposure times.

- Play with your camera settings and see what effects you can create. Night photography can be fun and incredibly creative.

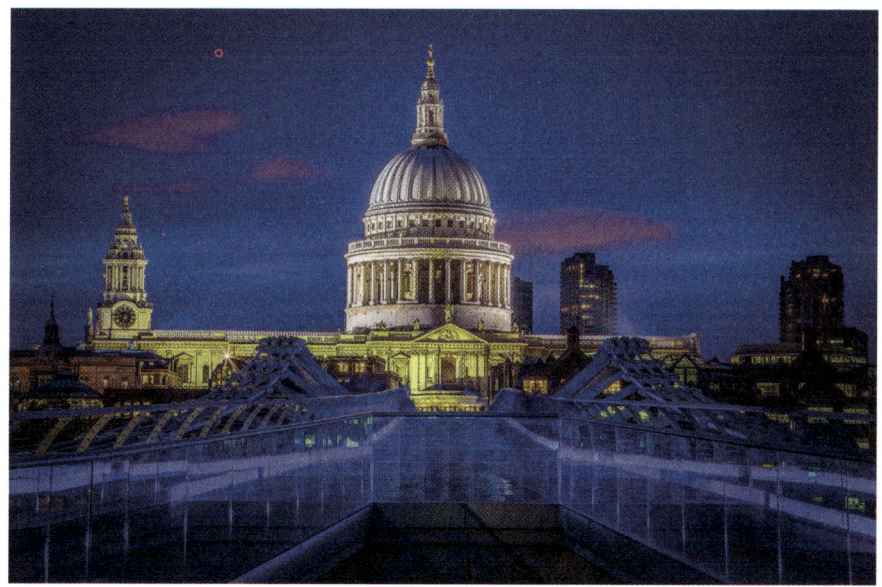

▲ *Photographing during the "blue hour" lets you include detail in the sky, along with the artificial lights of the city.*

TRAVEL NOTES

- Take care when photographing at night. Personal safety should always come first.

- The "blue hour" is a good time to photograph even when the weather isn't great.

- Moving carnival rides, night markets, neon signs, and traffic all make great subjects when shooting at night.

- Many cities are beside a river or ocean. The water can add an extra dimension by reflecting colorful lights.

- When photographing a cityscape, look for a viewpoint that shows off the skyline. This can sometimes be from outside the city or from the top of a tall building.

ASSIGNMENT 18

TECHNIQUE

- If a religious site is still being used for worship, show respect and try not to be disruptive:

    - Consider using a longer telephoto lens to shoot from a distance.

    - Use your camera's "silent shutter" mode if it has this option.

    - Increase the ISO if you are shooting a dark interior, rather than using a tripod.

    - Avoid using flash.

- Auto white balance may not produce accurate results, so shoot Raw so you can edit the colors in postproduction.

- Spot-metering mode is helpful if you are shooting through darker walkways into brighter areas.

TRAVEL NOTES

- What may appear foreign to you is an everyday occurrence to others, so remain aware and polite. Religion is a sensitive area and can lead to heated discussions and sometimes animosity. Always show respect.

- Research in advance what the culture permits or precludes with regard to photographing at religious sites. Check whether there are any restrictions on photographing at a particular site and always follow any specific rules.

- Ensure you dress appropriately and check to see if there are any requirements when entering a religious site, such as removing your shoes or covering your head.

PRO TIPS

- Think about focusing in on details, rather than capturing everything in one frame. Intricate carvings, stained glass, ornate artworks, statues, and symbols often adorn religious buildings, so make sure you capture these to reveal a sense of the place.

- A tilting screen on your camera can be useful for exploring different angles and perspectives.

CULTURE CLUB

You will most likely encounter some aspect of religion and faith wherever you go in the world. This can range from being the basis of an entire culture, to a more private and personal form of spirituality that is less easy to observe. Your mission here is to capture the concept of religion in your image. You may want to document how it has evolved over time and combined with age-old traditions and rituals or focus on the intimacy it creates with people and their beliefs in their gods.

Religious sites will offer up a wealth of photographic opportunities, with grand and imposing buildings containing myriad beautiful and intricate details. Religion may have influenced other key aspects of the local area as well, so you may notice that art, food, and clothing have all been affected. These will naturally provide you with other interesting, yet related, subjects for your images.

It is imperative on this assignment to maintain a strong sense of respect. Do not alienate or offend those using a temple or religious site just to obtain a photograph.

▼ *Churches are often adorned with ornate religious objects, grand architectural styling, and stained-glass windows that make great subject matter. Using a small aperture I was able to capture the bright sunlight with a starburst effect in this shot.*

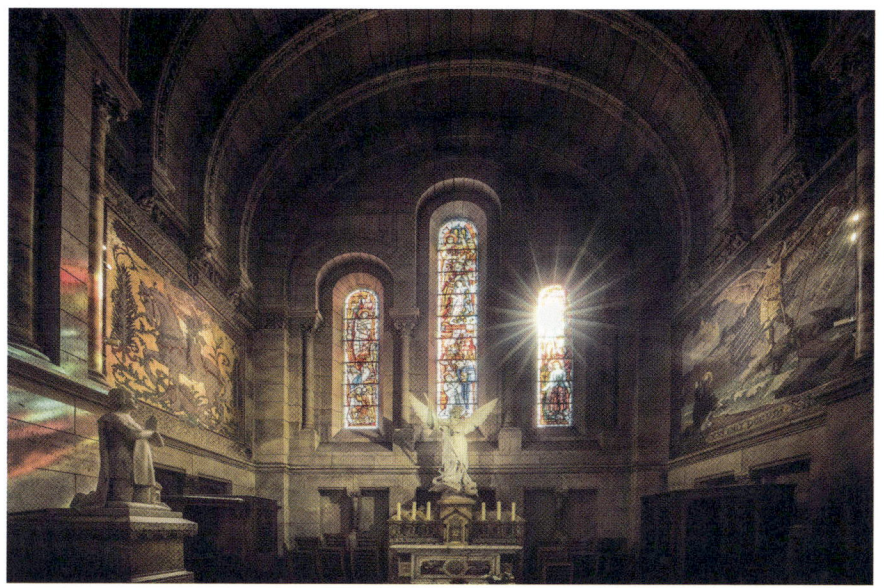

ASSIGNMENT

19

TECHNIQUE

- Look for patterns that you can emphasize. Filling the frame or cutting the pattern with the edge of the frame can create the impression that the pattern extends beyond the edges of the photograph.

- Breaking patterns is a strong compositional tool. Here, you fill a lot of the frame with a pattern, but then interrupt it, which adds natural interest to a viewer.

- You can emphasize a pattern by isolating it from its surroundings or contrasting it with areas of plain color.

TRAVEL PATTERNS

Patterns are all around us and can really help to create a dramatic and eye-catching image. Whether you find yourself out in nature or in a built-up urban environment, when you start to look you will soon see patterns more and more.

For this assignment the aim is to create a set of photographs that focus on a repeating pattern. Remember that patterns don't have to be in rows or lines—irregular formations can still create strong pattern-like tension in an image, such as a row of mountains or a few individual trees scattered around a landscape.

Look for repeating shapes, colors, or objects, and decide how you want to frame them—from the side, up high looking down, or up close and personal. Remember that the subject doesn't have to be immediately identifiable, as it is the reoccurring patterns that are the main focus of the image. For an additional challenge look for multiple patterns that can be included in the same shot.

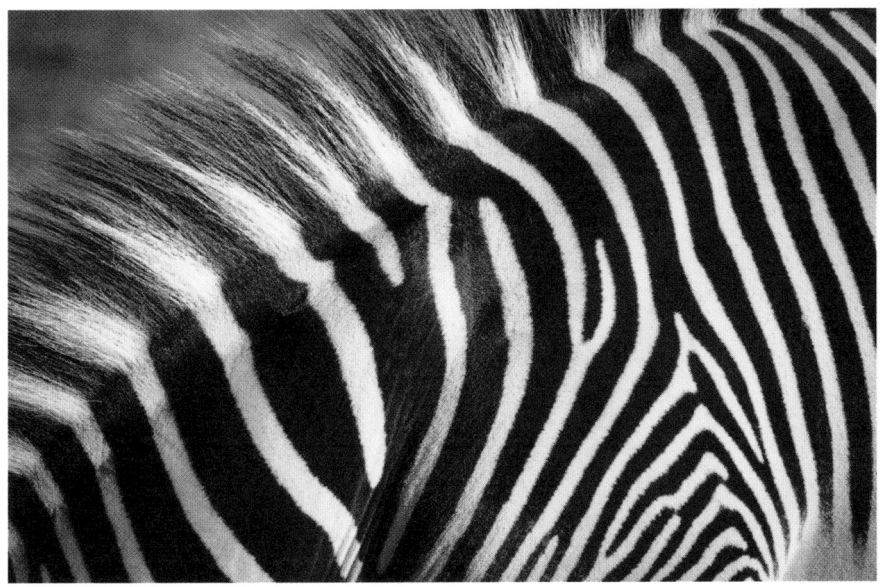

▲ *The natural world contains a lot of patterns, so make sure to look out for these when enjoying some time out in the wild.*

TRAVEL NOTES

- Man-made patterns are very common and you can find interesting examples in architecture, markets, industrial areas, and urban areas in general.

- Look for unique shapes and forms that relate to where you are and bring a well-defined theme to your images.

- Look around for patterns as you explore your location.

PRO TIPS

- Symmetry can create incredibly powerful compositions. Used in a considered way, images exhibit balance, proportion, and harmony between all of the elements.

- While symmetry is pleasing to the eye, the image can often look a little predictable if you don't have a strong focal point. Don't ignore your composition and subject matter.

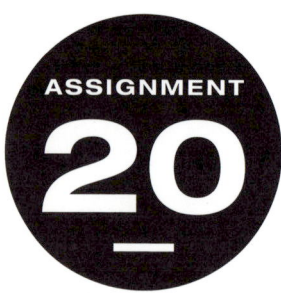

ASSIGNMENT

20

TECHNIQUE

- Your subject's environment will help you tell a lot of the story, so make sure you include some of the background in the image.

- The usual rules of composition remain important, so consider the position of your subject in the frame. The rule of thirds can be a good place to start if you are unsure.

- This image is unlikely to be posed, so try to set your camera in advance so you can capture the image first time, rather than risk missing the moment as you change the settings.

PRO TIPS

- Look for an interesting subject or a decisive moment in a scene that tells part of your subject's story.

- Consider whether to focus in on an element of your subject, such as their clothes or their hands, to reveal more about their daily life and routine.

TRAVEL NOTES

- People give life to images and tell you a little bit more about the culture you are in.

- Try to reveal a sense of your subject's "story." Think about what makes them unique and what angle will reveal more and help your viewer understand them.

- Consider finding a location and composition first, and then waiting for a suitable person to enter the frame to complete the image.

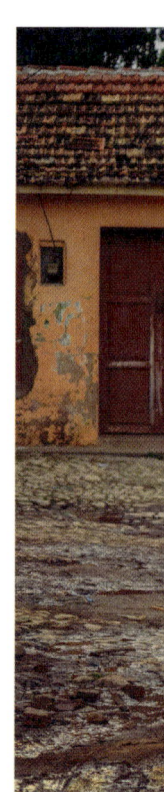

A MYSTERIOUS STRANGER

You can reveal a lot about where you are by including local people in your images. Through their clothes, jobs, or some other cultural aspect they can say a lot about the area you are traveling in and these interactions can also be some of the most rewarding parts of a trip.

With this assignment your aim is to try to capture the essence of a person and their location without showing their face. You want to create mystery and intrigue for your viewer and really make them think about the story behind the shot. Who is that person? What are they like? Where are they going? Where were you when you took the shot? The more questions your image raises the better.

▼ *I had to use a fast shutter speed to ensure that I captured a sharp image of this cowboy riding through a town. Including his surroundings raises questions about where he has been and where he is heading.*

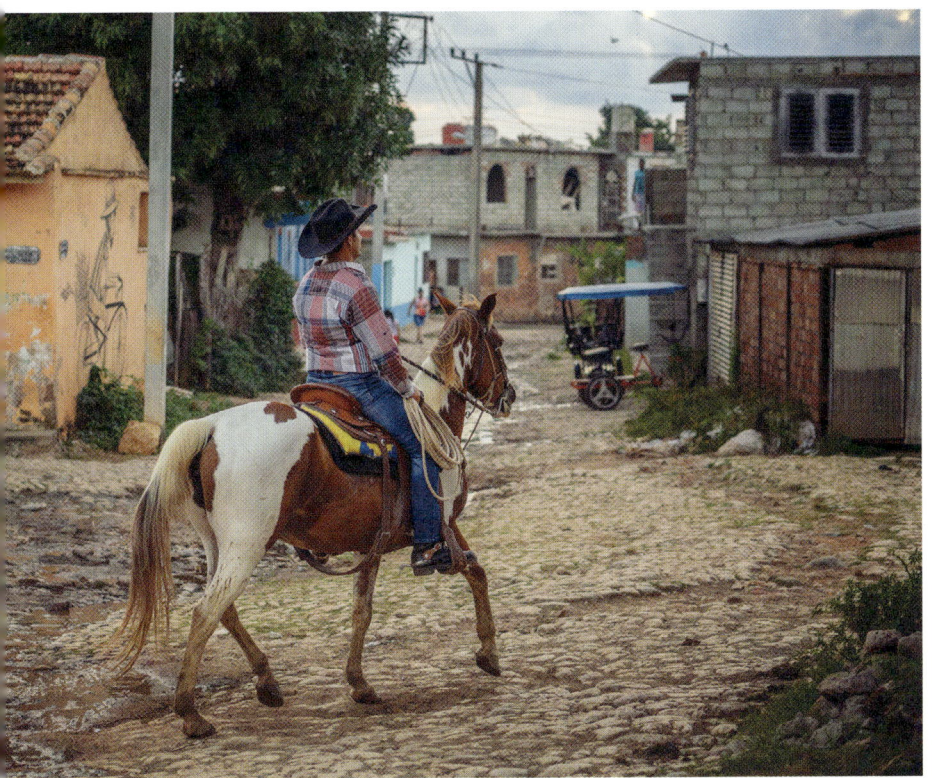

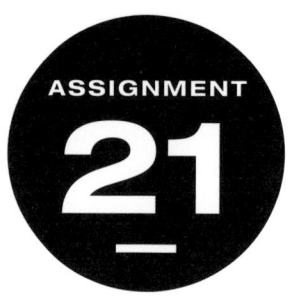

ASSIGNMENT

21

TECHNIQUE

- Play with the depth of field to determine whether the background appears in or out of focus.

- A wide aperture will help produce a bokeh effect on out-of-focus lights and bright highlights, which can create attractive backgrounds in your images.

- Using a tripod and remote release will help if you want to move your toy without changing your whole composition.

CRYSTAL BALL

Travel photography can become a little more fun and playful when you introduce your own toy, gimmick, or other element into the scene. The start of this assignment is to think of something to include in your images. Perhaps you want to buy a small toy replica of a landmark and place this in front of the image of the real thing? Alternatively, you might have something that you want to position in all your photographs to show that it is traveling with you and visiting all of the same places, such as a toy figure, car, dinosaur, or superhero.

You could also use a prop or other item creatively in front of the lens to change or improve your compositions. You could distort the view by wrapping your lens in clear plastic, for example, shoot through a tube or plastic bottle, or use a small mirror to reflect a scene. A popular item to consider using is a glass ball, or "crystal ball," as shown here.

ASSIGNMENT JOURNAL

_____   _____

_____   _____

_____   _____

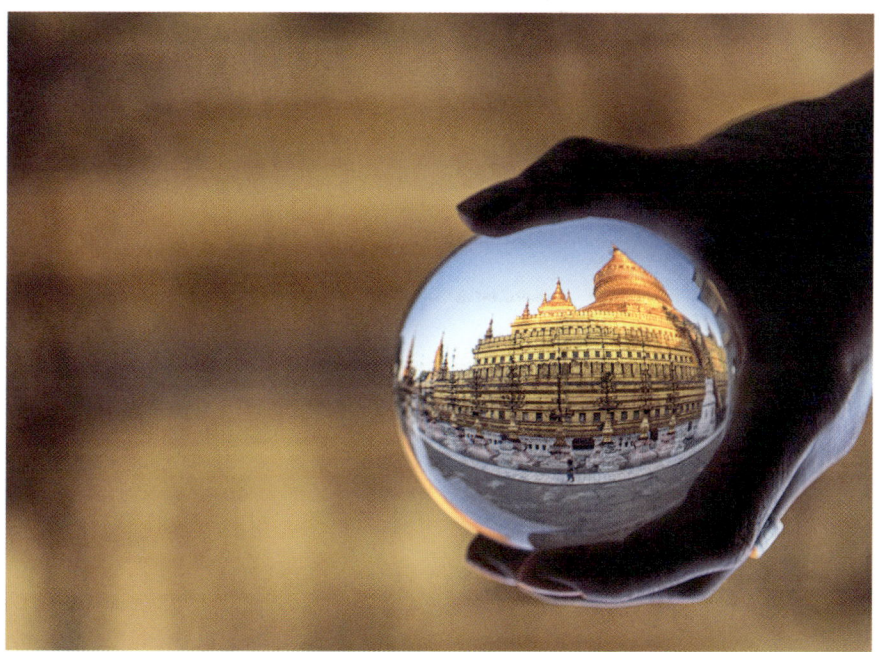

▲ *This image of a temple refracted in a crystal ball creates an intriguing and different take on what might otherwise just have been an "ordinary" image. As the refracted image was upside down, the photograph was flipped vertically in postproduction so it appeared the right way up.*

TRAVEL NOTES

- You could position your item in front of a whole range of travel backdrops and attractions to create a set of images.

- Consider putting your item into more mundane scenes to try to inject some humor into your images.

- There are some really interesting Instagram feeds focusing on the travels of certain toys. Consider setting up your own feed and documenting your toy's travels.

PRO TIPS

- Don't forget to look around and see if there is anything to hand that you can use creatively, such as a drinking glass or your sunglasses.

- If your camera's autofocus struggles to focus through your toy or other items, switch to manual focus instead.

- A toy car makes a great prop. You can play with angles, backgrounds, and force the perspective so it looks like it is on a road near a famous landmark or location.

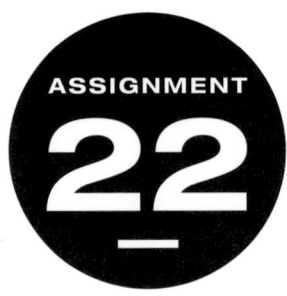

ASSIGNMENT

22

TECHNIQUE

- Choosing the right aperture is important. Use a wide aperture to help blur the frame and make it less distracting, or a smaller aperture to ensure that both your frame and subject appear sharp.

- Getting the correct exposure can be tricky, especially if you are inside and the subject is brightly lit outside. Spot-metering mode can help or you can dial in negative exposure compensation.

- You still have to consider your overall composition and where you want to place your subject.

TRAVEL NOTES

- You will naturally encounter a lot of potential frames in architecture. Doorways, entrance halls, windows, and corridors can all be used to frame interesting subjects.

- The more you look, the more you will see potential framing opportunities. Car, bus, and shop windows—even boat portholes—can strengthen a composition and add intrigue to a view, whether you're looking inside or out.

- You can find equally strong elements in nature, such as a jungle canopy or clearing, a rocky outcrop or overhang, caves, clouds, or other formations.

▶ *The ruined walls of an old church provided the perfect frame for this large stone cross, adding mood and interest to the image.*

PRO TIPS

- Ask yourself if the inclusion of a frame helps make a stronger image. Not all compositions or subjects benefit from this technique.

- Consider whether the frame adds to the story. Does it provide context or enhance the focal point?

- A partial or implied frame can often be very effective—you don't need a solid frame that goes around all four edges of the image.

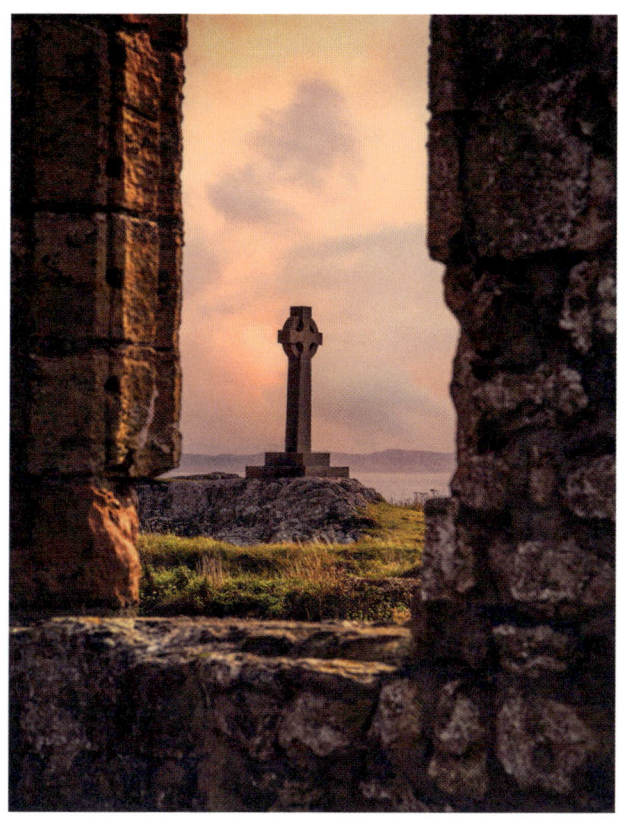

YOU'VE BEEN FRAMED

Walk into any art gallery or museum and you will see that almost all the pictures—whether they are paintings or photographs—are mounted in frames on the walls. These frames create a border that naturally directs where the viewer is supposed to look.

Similarly, framing your subject within a composition is also a really strong way of focusing attention on a specific area or part of your photograph. You will find that having a boundary will keep your viewer's gaze from moving away from the subject. A frame also has the effect of making your images seem more three-dimensional, as you are looking through one layer into another.

The idea for this assignment is to frame your subject within the image. Look for a natural way to do this when you choose your composition: it could be a physical frame like a doorway or arch, a natural element such as trees and branches, or even an implied frame created by reflections or rocks.

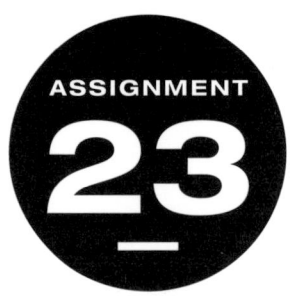

ASSIGNMENT 23

TECHNIQUE

- Composition is key here. It might be tricky to retain your preferred composition and have your scale element in shot, so be prepared to compromise. Consider moving around and looking for different viewpoints to see if this helps.

- Your lens choice will impact your ability to show scale. A telephoto lens will appear to compress a scene and flatten perspective, while a wideangle lens will emphasize foreground elements and make background details appear smaller.

ASSIGNMENT JOURNAL

TRAVEL NOTES

- Vast landscapes can easily appear underwhelming without a point of reference, so look for a person, animal, or other structure that can help gauge size.

- Large urban landmarks will be popular with tourists and other travelers so consider including them to reveal more of the true scale of something.

PRO TIPS

- Try to balance the objects in the scene and decide what is necessary to help suggest size.

- Playing with your angle of view can change the perspective and emphasize different parts of your image.

▶ *It was hard to appreciate the true size of the mountain range in front of me and looking at my initial images I was a little underwhelmed. I took a few paces to alter my position and reframed the shot to include the church, which provides a sense of scale.*

CLIMB ANY MOUNTAIN

Quite often when you are exploring, you will find yourself in front of a spectacular view or something incredibly large and dramatic. A common problem is that when you return home you can find that your photographs really don't do the scene justice—the image just doesn't convey the scale of the structure or view. This is because it can be hard to retain a sense of size and significance in a two-dimensional image.

An easy way to indicate the true size of something is to include something else in the shot that can help your viewer interpret relative sizes. This could be a person, or something man-made or natural that your audience will understand the size of, so they can subconsciously compare it to the other elements in your image.

Your assignment is to try to capture the true scale of something huge, such as a grand landscape or giant structure, by including a reference point in the image that reveals its true size. Think about what you can see in the scene that you can include to help give the impression of enormity and show your viewers how extraordinary the sight really was.

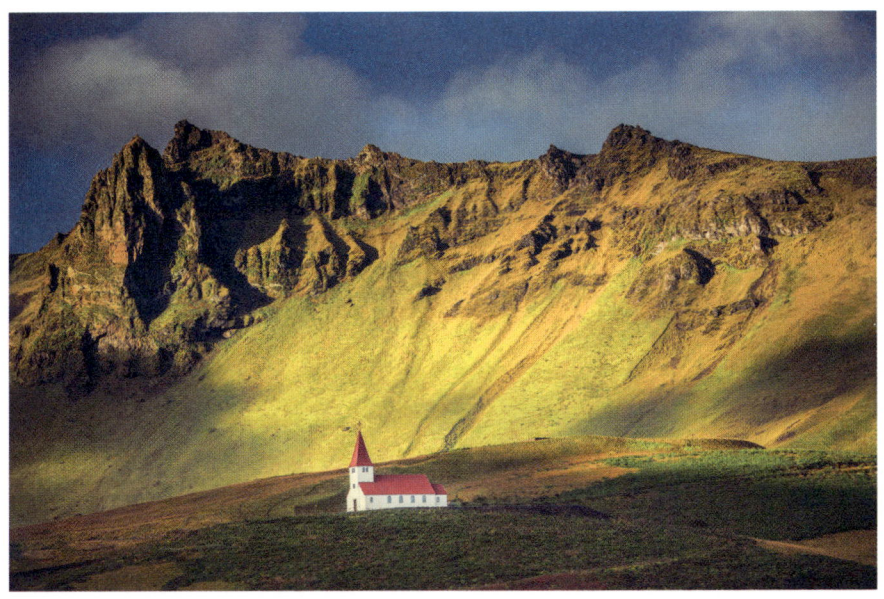

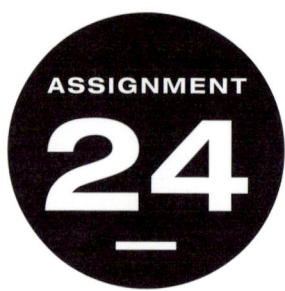

ASSIGNMENT

24

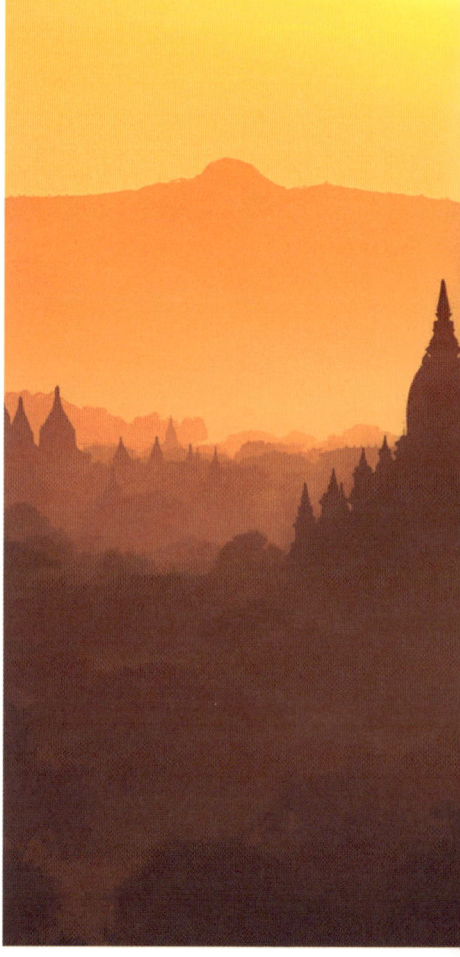

▼ *These backlit temples in Myanmar create a beautiful silhouetted scene at sunset. Setting the exposure for the bright sky (and not including the sun) meant that the darker areas fell further into shadow, creating a strong silhouetted image.*

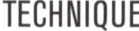

TECHNIQUE

- Set your ISO as low as possible and manually expose for the highlights.

- If you are using an automatic exposure mode your camera will try to average out the light in a scene, making your silhouette brighter than it should be. Use negative exposure compensation to counter this.

- Your camera might struggle to focus automatically so manual focus may be easier. Look for the edges of contrasting areas to help you achieve sharp focus.

SILHOUETTED

You may have heard photographers talking about not shooting into the sun, but when the backlight can be controlled you can create some striking silhouettes. The aim of this assignment is to do exactly that: to create the "perfectly silhouetted image."

To achieve this you need to focus on three important elements. First, you need to find a suitable source of backlighting, whether it's a sunset, a bright window or doorway, the moon, neon lights, bright signage, or just the light at the end of a hallway. Whatever it is, you need a strong light source that you can use to frame your subject. You can see the creative possibilities here and on pages 64–5.

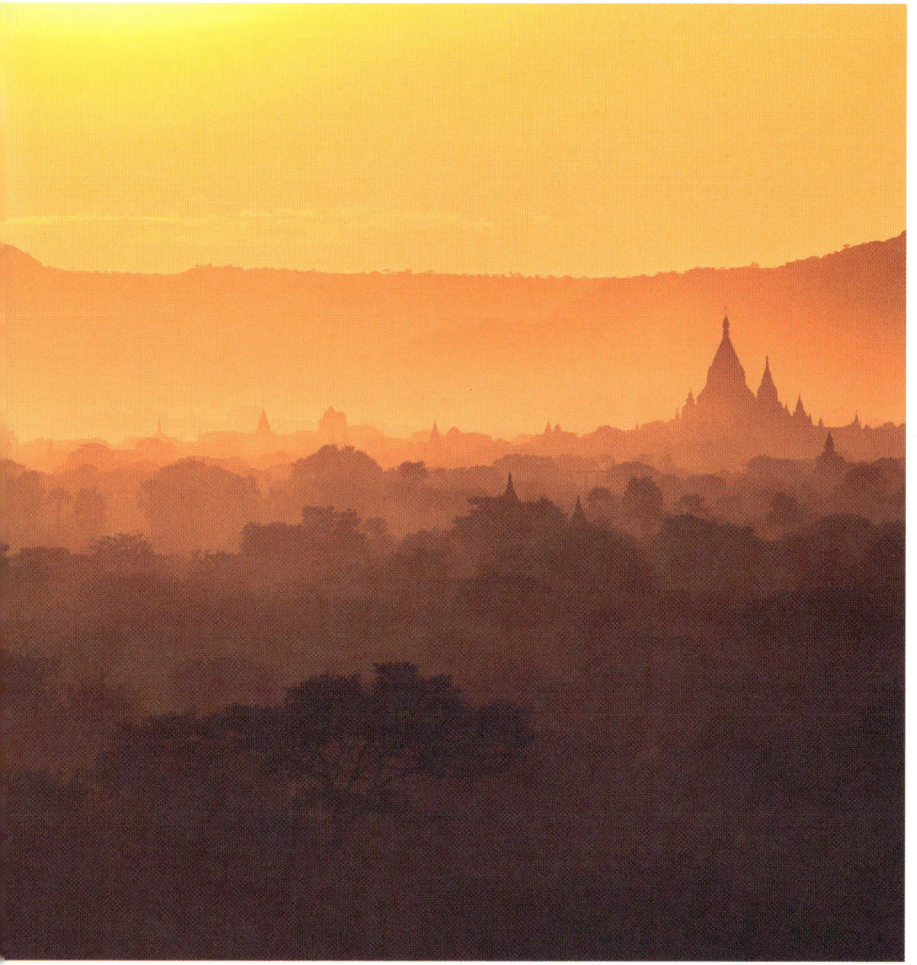

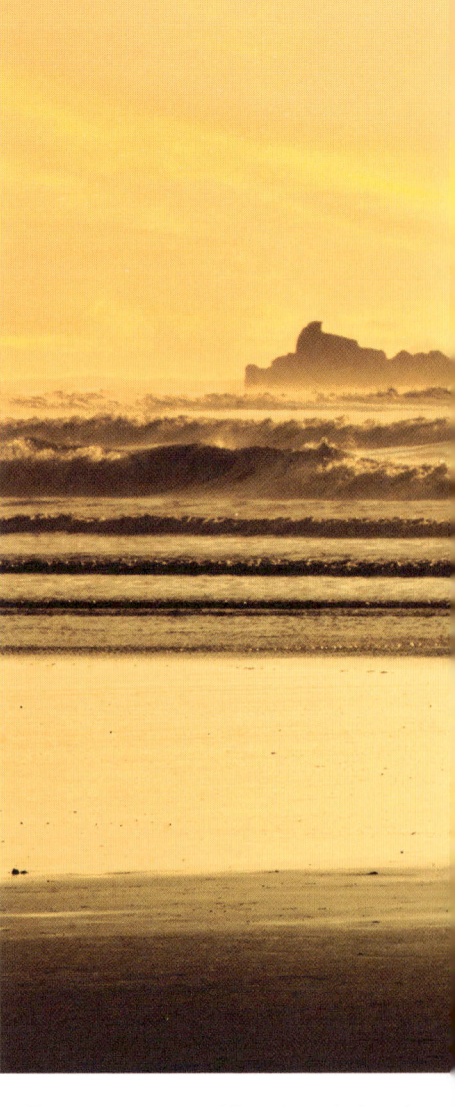

▲ *This horseman was riding along the beach as the sun was starting to set. A relatively fast shutter speed froze the motion of the horse and rider, and being backlit they fell into a perfect silhouette.*

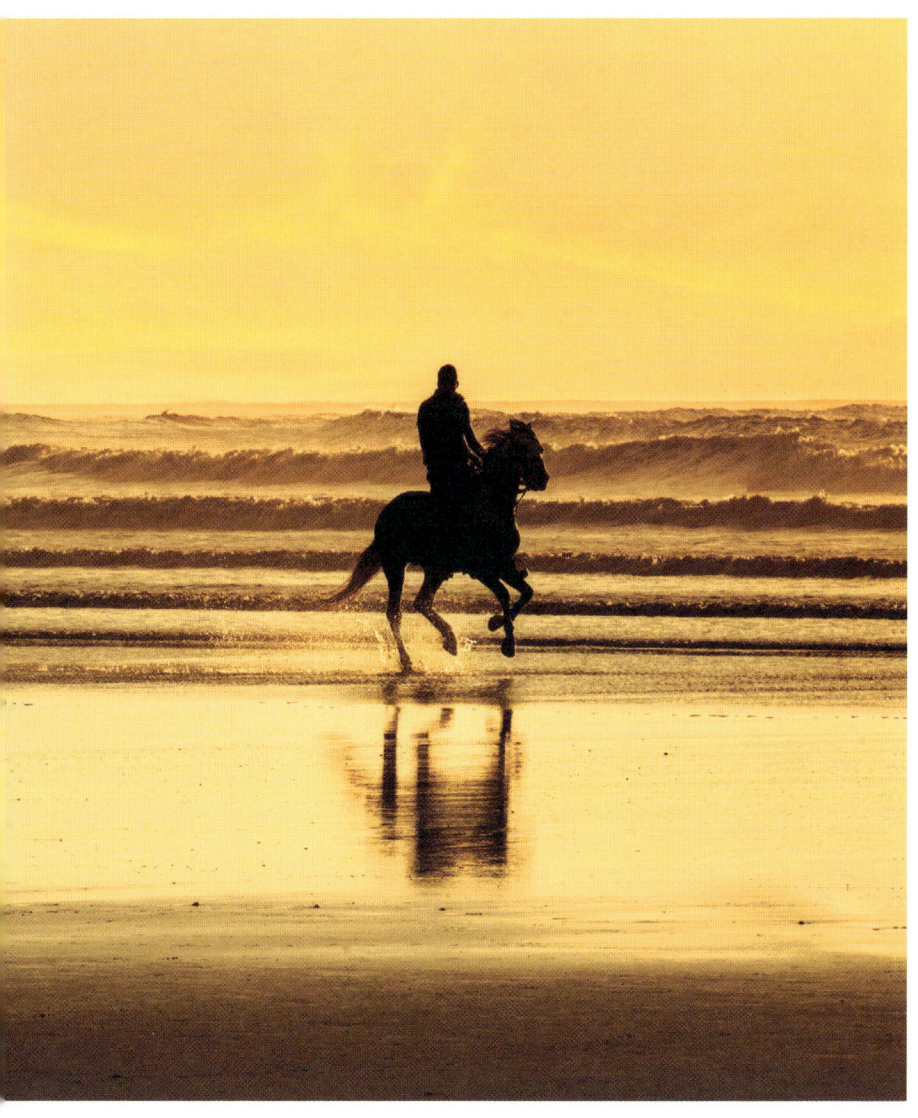

The subject is the next vital ingredient to creating a vivid silhouette. Choose your subject carefully, as it will be thrown into darkness and its outline will be solely responsible for revealing what it is. Bold, identifiable objects that have a distinctive shape work well here.

The final element is the composition. Where your subject is in the frame and how it works with the backlight is the key to making an intriguing and strong image, so explore different angles and lenses to make the best shot you can.

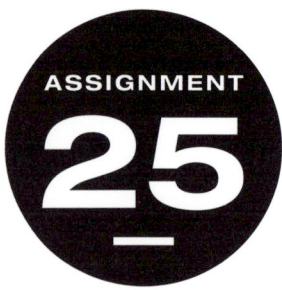

TECHNIQUE

- Strong light will create strong shadows.

- When the sun or light source is at a low angle, shadows become longer, which can create interesting compositions.

- A small light source will create hard shadows, whereas a light source that is large or far away will create softer shadows with graduated edges.

- Chiaroscuro describes the relationship between light and dark, where less critical aspects of the scene are left to fall into shadow and highlights accentuate the important elements.

▼ *The sunlight cast a small amount of light on the upper balconies in this backstreet tenement building. The graduation of light between the brighter areas and the darker shadows helps strengthen the mood.*

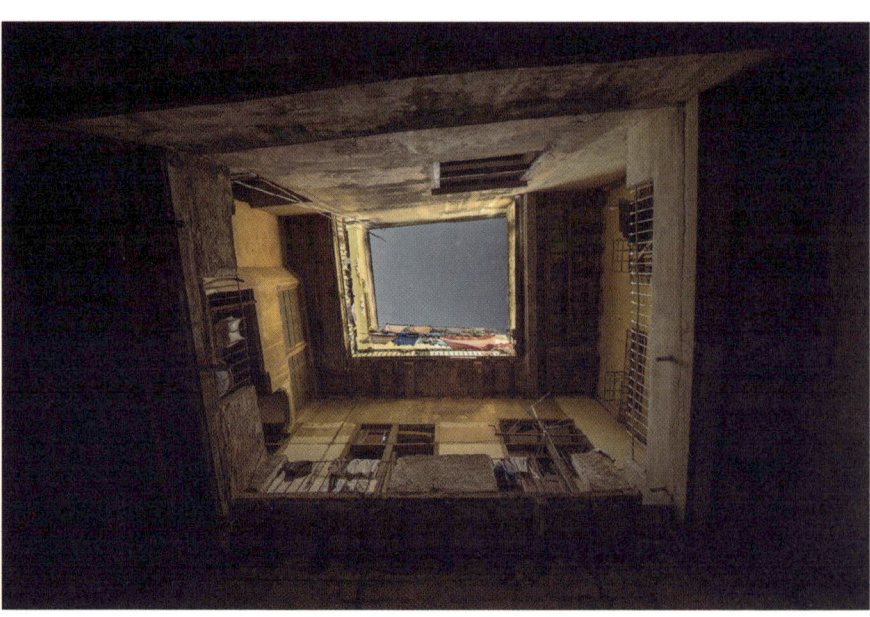

IN THE SHADOWS

Shadows follow everything on a bright sunny day and under strong artificial lighting, providing contrast and helping to give shape and dimension to the world around us. Used on their own or as part of a wider image, strong shadows can draw your viewer's attention and help to create powerful photographs.

For this assignment you need to create an image that uses shadows to enhance it. You might decide to use shadows to balance your main subject or as the subject itself, but think about how you can use them to your artistic advantage. You could also use them to direct your viewer's attention, by concealing details that are less important to the image.

▼ *You can make interesting abstract photographs using shadows, as they can accentuate shape and form. The strong midday light in this shot created strong shadows from the metal fire escapes.*

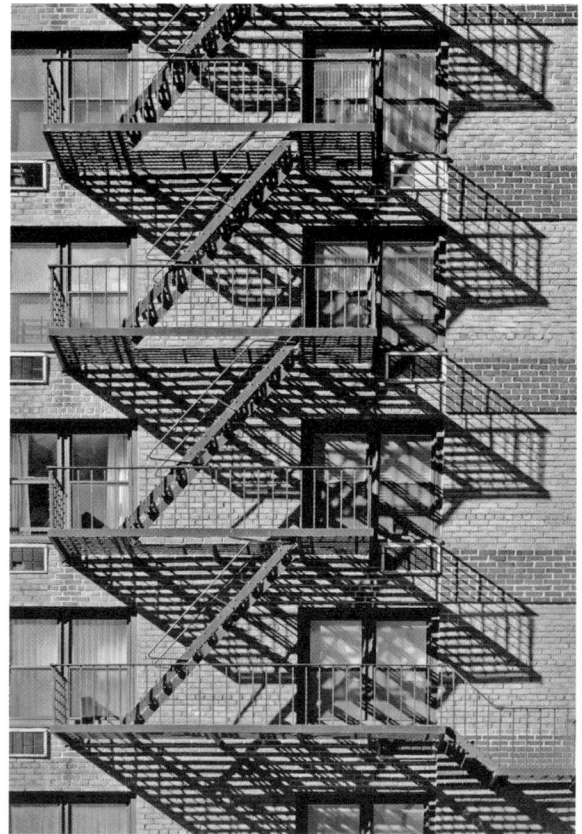

PRO TIPS

- Consider converting your images to black and white. This reinforces the gray tones that make up the shadows and removes any contrasting hues that might compete for attention.

- Artificial lights can make interesting shadows and throw colored light onto your scene, especially at night.

- Too many competing shadows can over-complicate a scene and become a distraction.

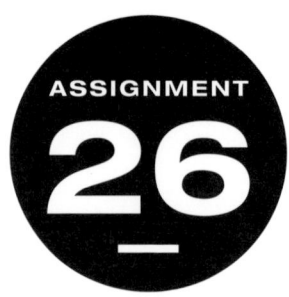

ASSIGNMENT

26

TECHNIQUE

- Most images require a foreground, middle ground, and background, so consider where to include your visual clues.

- Composition is critical, as you still want to create an interesting image, so think about how you can incorporate the clues.

- If you are photographing a flag that is moving in the wind, you may need to use a fast shutter speed and split-second timing to capture it when it is in the right position and unfurled.

▶ *This signpost in the Florida Keys really captures the essence of where I was. The tropical palms and distance information served as a pleasant reminder for this part of my trip, as well as revealing my location to my audience.*

SIGNPOSTING

Some images you take while traveling will be "location anonymous," as your viewer won't necessary know where you were in the world when you took it. It may be a beach, a mountain range, or an urban street, but without some sort of visual clue it can be hard for your audience to know where you were when you took the shot.

This assignment is to take an image in a particular place that gives a direct clue as to where you were. You can decide how prominent or subtle you want your hint to be. You might choose to make it instantly clear where you were by including a famous landmark, flag, street sign, or the destination on the front of a bus. Alternatively, you might want to make your viewers work a little bit harder, with advertising, the way people are dressed, or their mode of transport providing the clues. In either case, the key is to look around and identify what makes the area you're in unique compared to other areas or countries.

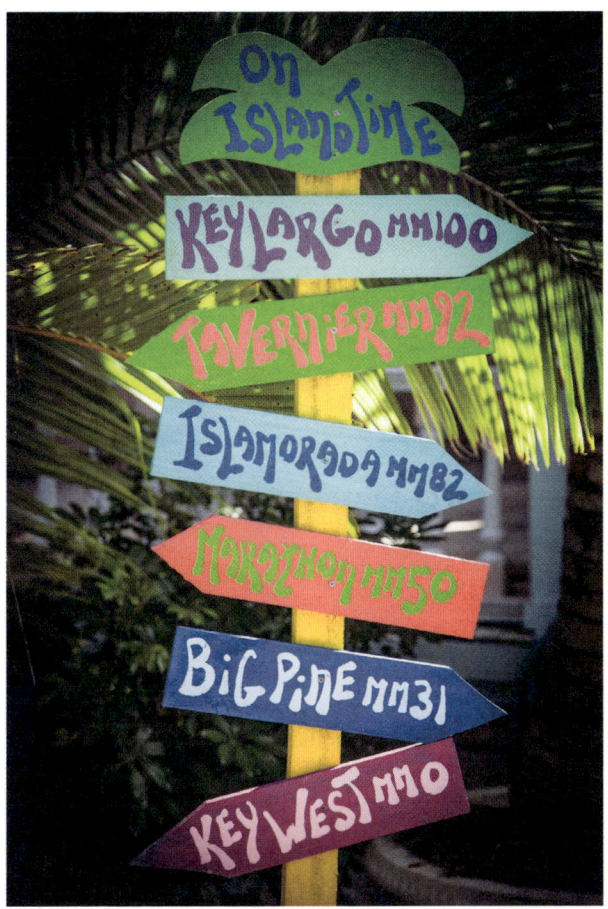

TRAVEL NOTES

- Every country has a flag that evokes pride and strong feeling. Make sure you respect this and do not do anything that might cause offence.

- Including identifiable elements will make it easier to remember the location where an image was taken.

- Think about including local animals, viewpoints, vegetation, or food that is commonly associated with your particular location.

- Graffiti, advertising, and posters will all provide clues that help reveal your whereabouts.

PRO TIPS

- Consider where to place the information in your image—don't just document a sign in an obvious position or up close.

- As you explore your location you will see more elements that reveal clues about where you are.

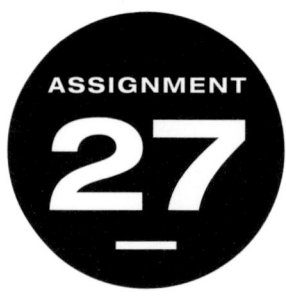

TECHNIQUE

- A fast shutter speed will freeze any motion in water, while a slower shutter speed will create a dreamy blur.

- Filters can help when photographing water. A polarizing filter can reduce glare and reflections, while neutral density (ND) filters extend the exposure time.

- It is easy to overexpose the highlights, so be prepared to apply a small amount of negative exposure compensation.

- Consider using a telephoto lens if you don't want to get too close to the water itself or you are photographing water sports.

PRO TIPS

- Protect your camera around water. A plastic bag or rain cover should be used if it is raining and you might want to consider a dry bag or other waterproof container while you are transporting your kit.

- Be extremely careful around water. Slippery rocks, deep or fast-moving water, and large waves can all catch you out.

- Consider capturing sunlit foliage reflected at the water's edge, or include an interesting foreground element sticking out of a natural water source, such as a boulder or log.

- An interesting curve or meander can add a leading line to your composition.

- If you're working at the coast, always check the tide times and make sure you won't be cut off.

TRAVEL NOTES

- Taking a boat trip will give you an opportunity to shoot more unique water-based compositions.

- Fishing docks and fishermen can provide interesting subject matter around water, and will add some local flavor to your shots.

- Aquariums can be great places for interesting photography, but it can be tricky to get the correct white balance. Shooting Raw is a good option.

- A waterproof camera or housing will let you to shoot underwater, adding another dimension to your shots.

GO WITH THE FLOW

Water covers more than 70 percent of the Earth's surface, so it is found almost everywhere we go. It is an essential life ingredient and a powerful force of nature, so it goes without saying that photographing water in its many forms can make a beautiful image.

Your task here is to create an image where water—in any form—is the main focal point or subject. Decide how you want to capture it and what message you want to convey. You could include it as a small point of interest in a wideangle image or it could fill the frame. Whatever path you take, don't forget that water also triggers a wide range of emotions ranging from peace and tranquility to power and drama, depending on its location, size, and flow.

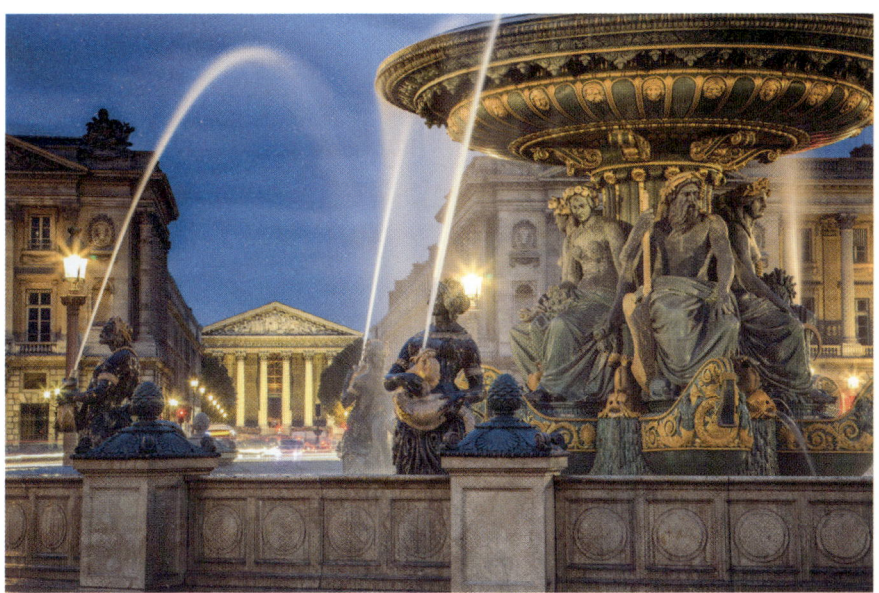

▲ Water fountains can make interesting architectural subjects, especially when they are as ornately detailed as this one. Using a slow shutter speed and a tripod, I was able to capture the water together with the city lights.

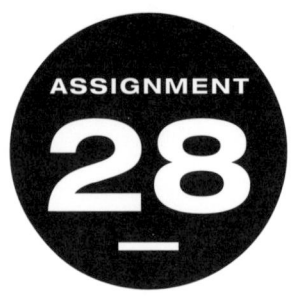

ASSIGNMENT

28

TECHNIQUE

- Use a fast shutter speed if you are shooting from a moving vehicle so that you freeze motion and end up with a sharp image.

- Continuous drive mode will increase the chance of a sharp frame being captured in a sequence.

- If possible, use image stabilization on your camera or lens to keep your shots sharply focused.

ROAD TRIP

Quite often, your journey can be as important as reaching your destination. Maybe your adventure starts when you travel to the airport or railway station, or perhaps you are going on an actual road trip and the voyage itself is the basis of your expedition.

Either way, your mission here is to document your "road trip" with a set of between eight and ten images that capture the essence of your adventure. You should try to record the sense of freedom and excitement that this part of the voyage brings. Make sure to include your chosen mode of transport, as this will reveal to your audience how you chose to travel. Look for landmarks and other points of interest that show where you were headed and document the various elements of your trip—the people you met, what you saw out of the window, where you were sitting, what it was like inside your transport, and anything else unique and out of the ordinary. Finish with images that summarize the trip, showing where you ended up, what the trip meant to you, and how it made you feel.

ASSIGNMENT JOURNAL

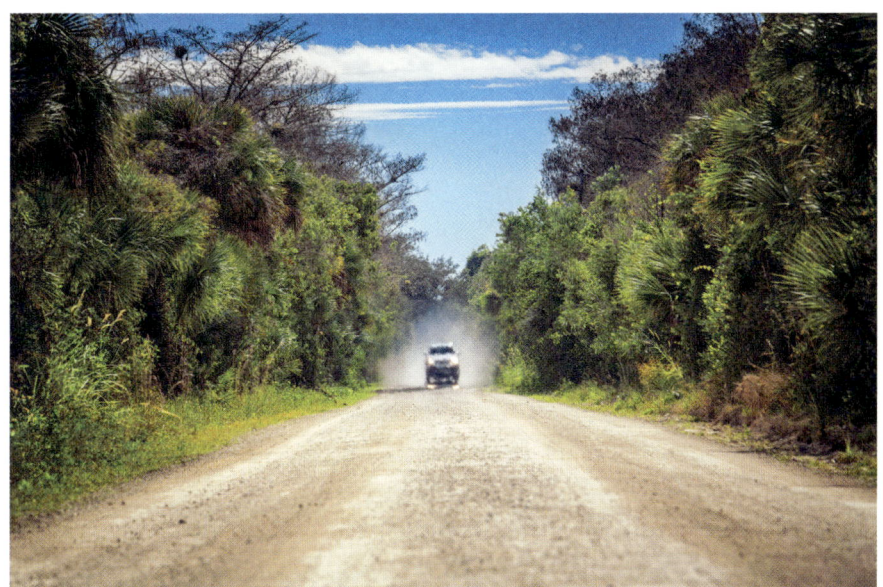

▲ *Make sure you include the local environment in your images. Having the road or path in shot will make it clearer to your viewers where you were.*

TRAVEL NOTES

- A lot of the interesting aspects of a journey will be in the details. Don't just capture the scenery, but also the seemingly mundane or common tasks, such as filling up with gas or buying supplies, as these will help tell more of a story about your trip.

- If you can, take your time to travel slowly and explore. Stop off every now and again to see what you can discover. Give yourself plenty of time to get to your destination, so you don't have to rush.

- You will want to capture a sense of place in your images, but don't focus so much on the location that you forget to capture the journey.

- A human dimension can add interest to this assignment, revealing the people who live and work along the route you have chosen to travel.

PRO TIPS

- Keep your camera ready to capture unusual signs, or other intriguing elements that you pass as you travel.

- You can usually carry a little more gear if traveling in a vehicle, so take advantage of this.

- It can be useful to have a "grab bag" containing your camera, lens, and a spare battery and memory card, so everything you need is to hand when you stop during your journey.

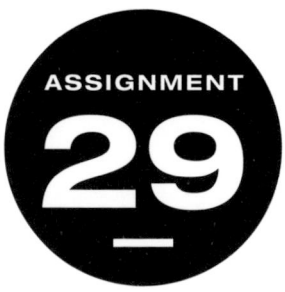

ASSIGNMENT

29

TECHNIQUE

- The light will change quickly on days when it is windy with broken cloud, so keep an eye on your exposure settings. You may have to adjust these regularly to adapt to the changeable light.

- Snow can confuse your camera's exposure meter, resulting in "gray" images. Use positive exposure compensation to boost the exposure and ensure the white snow is captured correctly.

- Keep microfiber cloths on hand to keep your lens and filters clean.

- Consider using a fast shutter speed to freeze falling rain or snow.

- Use a lens hood on a rainy day to help protect your lens from water droplets.

TRAVEL NOTES

- Reflections can result in beautiful photographs on rainy days (see Assignment 01).

- Check the weather forecast so you don't get caught out in any extreme heat, snow, or downpours.

- Watch out for lightning and other electrical storms. Take appropriate cover where necessary.

- Carry water, a hat, and sunblock if you are going to be out for long periods in intense sunshine.

- Preparation is key. Ensure you are protected from the elements, as there is nothing more miserable than being cold or wet.

PRO TIPS

- Ensure your camera is protected from the rain, as water and electronics don't mix well.

- Cold temperatures will affect your camera's battery life. Carry a spare in an inside jacket pocket to keep it warm and help it last a little longer.

- Moving from cool to hot environments can create condensation on your lens, so check this when moving from an air-conditioned interior out into the heat of the sun, or heading into the warm when it's cold outside.

RAIN OR SHINE

Wherever you end up on your travels, you are likely to encounter unpredictable weather. Sure, if you take a trip to an equatorial desert you will likely only face intense heat, and in the mountains in winter the extremes of wind and snow, but in most other locations the weather is more variable. Don't let this stop you taking your camera out and about, as you will often find that a change of weather can help you capture some captivating photographs.

Your assignment is to head out in "bad" weather to capture images that show how your location is affected by different conditions. Perhaps there is intense snowfall or strong winds that you want to capture, or stormy skies that create moody images full of drama and contrast. Rainy days can be a little harder, and it is vital that you keep your camera dry, but don't let that put you off—an umbrella will help, and you can also look for sheltered areas to shoot from and stay dry.

▼ *A cold winter rainstorm is nothing new in London, England, but it's not something that should prevent you from venturing out. It can create a lovely reflective sheen on some surfaces (especially at night), but watch out for too many raindrops hitting your lens.*

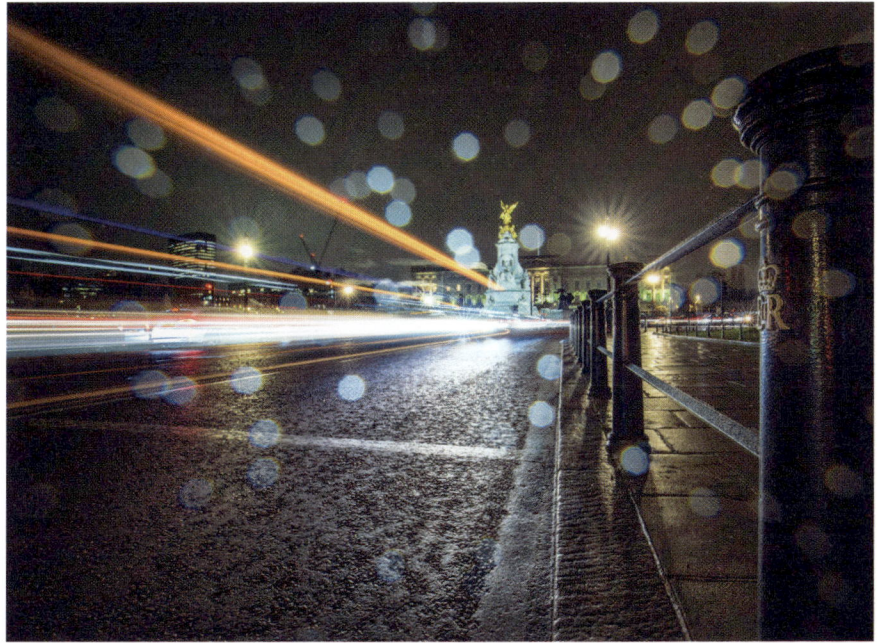

ASSIGNMENT

30

TECHNIQUE

- If you can get close to the action, consider using a wideangle lens to exaggerate the proportions of the scene and the subject.

- A fast shutter speed can freeze the action, while a slow shutter speed can help convey a sense of movement.

- Your camera's burst (or drive) mode will improve your chances of capturing the strongest and sharpest image, by giving you a range of shots to choose from.

- Increase your ISO when shooting in low-light conditions.

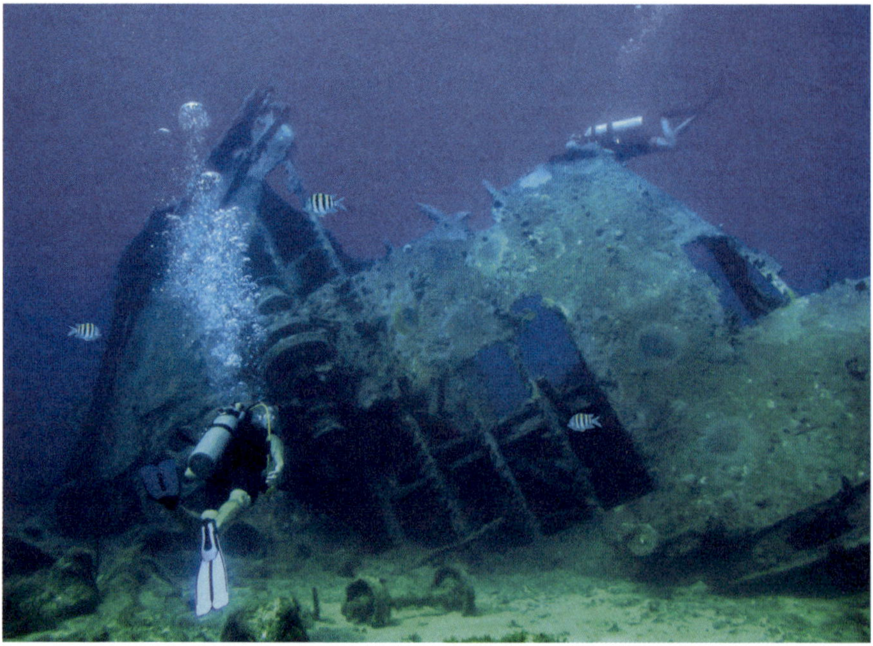

ADRENALINE RUSH

You will often have the opportunity to experience or observe "extreme" sports when you are traveling, with an underlying sense of adrenaline and danger. This makes them an exciting subject for photography, and the focus of this assignment.

Set out to capture an image that involves some element of adventure sports. It may be that you are going to participate yourself and want to capture your involvement in the activity, or you can capture someone else taking part. In either case, the objective is to try to capture the energy and excitement, and to produce a really dynamic image (or set of images). The action is going to be fast-paced, so try to think ahead about what you want to capture and what settings you'll need on your camera. You should also be imaginative with your angles—shooting from low down can really help to make the subject imposing in the frame, for example, but consider other angles as well.

TRAVEL NOTES

- Check that your insurance covers you and your gear if you are participating in extreme sports.

- This can be a good time to capture your friends in action if you don't want to participate yourself.

- Try to include a sense of place in your background, as this will add an additional layer of interest and context for your viewers.

PRO TIPS

- Compositionally, decide whether to leave space around your subject so there is room for the action, or close in and fill the frame for a strong, powerful composition.

- A telephoto lens will help you get close to the action if you can't physically move in closer or it is dangerous to do so.

- Consider pre-focusing your shot if you know the subject will be in a certain position. This will help you take a picture faster, as there's no delay while the camera focuses.

- Don't just shoot the peak of the action. Consider the in-between moments, as they will help tell the broader story and capture the atmosphere.

- Ensure your gear is protected from the elements, especially dust, sand, and sea spray. Afterward, clean your equipment as soon as you can.

◀ *A waterproof housing for your camera is a great way of protecting it from the elements and also opens up a wealth of opportunities for different and unique photographs, such as this shot, which was taken during an underwater wreck dive.*

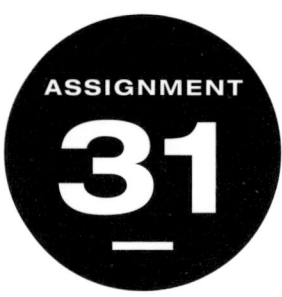

ASSIGNMENT

31

TECHNIQUE

- A wideangle lens will allow you to fit more of a building in the frame, but will also distort its shape. The wider the focal length, the more pronounced the distortion will be.

- You can use slow shutter speeds (with a tripod), but use an aperture of at least f/8 to make sure you have sufficient depth of field to capture the building sharply.

- The time of day you choose to shoot will affect your images, as the angle of light can change the look and feel of a building. Play with shadows and light to emphasize or flatten shape and form.

PRO TIPS

- Consider including people to provide a sense of scale and perspective. Including people can also make images more attractive to your viewers.

- If you are focusing on details, look for distinctive shapes, repeating patterns, symmetry, or examples of intricate and ornate craftsmanship that are pleasing to the eye.

- It can sometimes be challenging to find a good composition, as you have no control over the position of the subject, so make sure you walk around and try different angles.

TRAVEL NOTES

- Try to capture buildings that show the essence of the area you are visiting. Look for the strong religious and cultural influences that have led to their unique style.

- Most cities will have an old town and a more modern center or business district. Visit both to get a real sense of the place.

- Don't forget to shoot images at night, as the way that some buildings are lit can really create dynamic images.

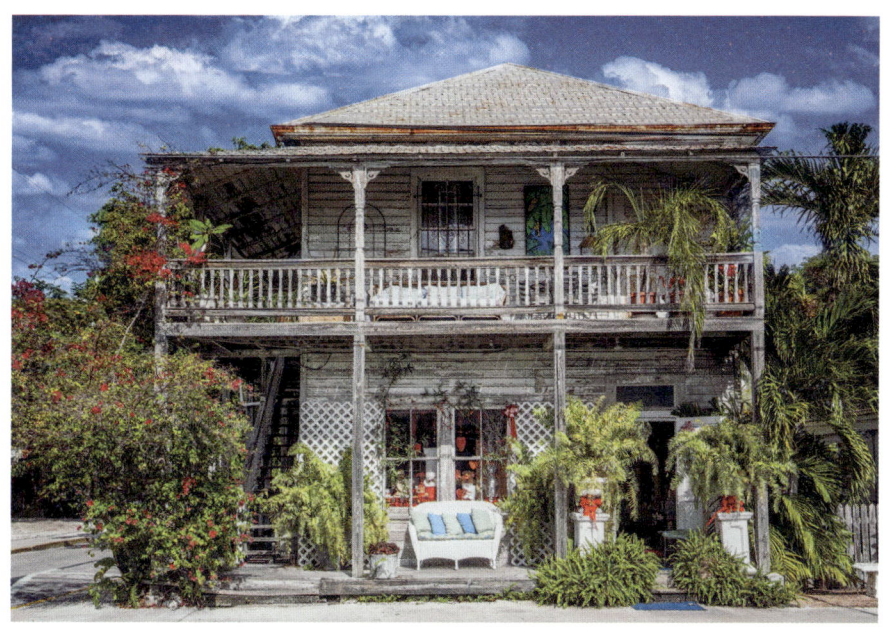

▲ *Architecture can represent where you were and reveal a little more about the area you were visiting.*

ARCHITECTURE TOUR

The architecture at your destination can be unique and significant. What you see around you will naturally have been influenced by local tradition, culture, religion, and other social aspects over different points in history.

For this assignment, your aim is to create a set of six images that capture three old and three more modern buildings or structures in a particular place, so you get a flavor of the different architectural styles that have been adopted over time.

However, don't just point and shoot. You want to try to capture the true essence of the building, whether that means focusing in on the craftsmanship, ornate details, or some other important aspect of it. Play with your angle of view and composition to try to create unique images that capture the soul of the structure in a less obvious way. Walk around to find different vantage points and think about how you can show off the architecture in its best light.

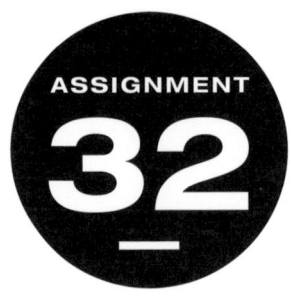

ASSIGNMENT

32

TECHNIQUE

- A telephoto lens allows you to shoot from a distance, which will not only help you get closer to your subject, but also cut out any distracting elements.

- A macro lens will let you fill the frame with smaller animals or insects.

- As with any portrait, ensure that you focus on your subject's eye and that it is sharp.

- A fast shutter speed will help freeze any movement, which can be especially useful when photographing birds in flight.

- A wide aperture can help isolate an animal from its background and reduce the visibility of bars from fences if you are photographing at a sanctuary or zoo.

ON SAFARI

Wherever you are traveling to, you will likely find that the natural world is very different to your home environment. There may be a whole range of animals and other wildlife that is unique to your travel destination, so your brief here is to focus on something that you don't normally see in your own local area. This could range from large predators all the way through to smaller creatures, such as birds, lizards, or even insects. Decide whether you want to take a portrait of the animal, show it in its natural environment, or reveal its relationship with other animals or its surroundings, and aim to produce a small series of images that work well together.

ASSIGNMENT JOURNAL

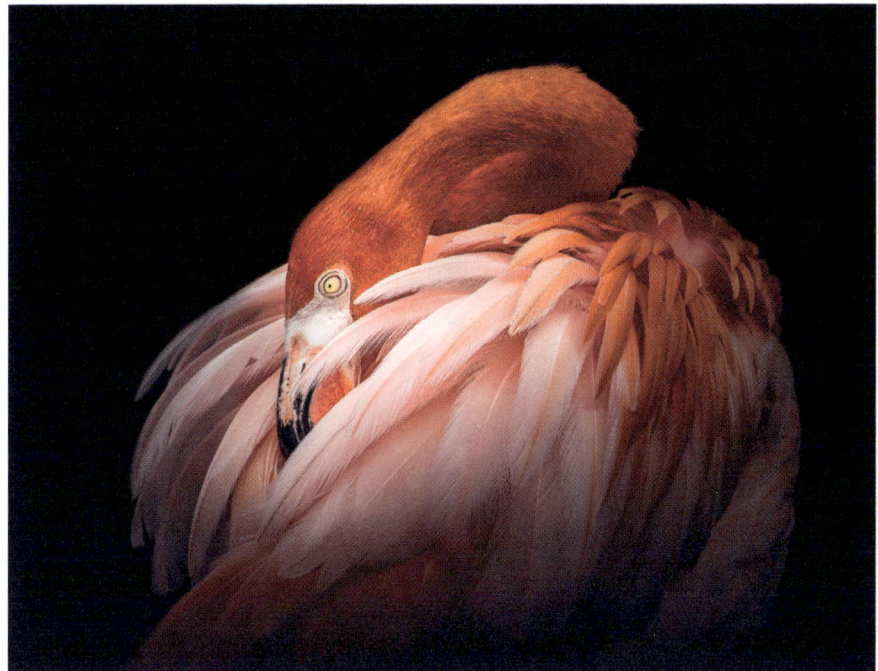

▲ *Get low and try to take your images from the animal's eye level, rather than your own. This will make a stronger photograph that seems to connect more with the subject.*

PRO TIPS

- Take care not to startle or aggravate your wildlife subject. Animals will make themselves pretty clear if they feel threatened or annoyed.

- Consider photographing just part of the animal. Smaller details, such as fur or feathers, can reveal some of nature's beauty that your viewers will find interesting.

TRAVEL NOTES

- Some animals are unique to a place, so try to ensure that you can see (and photograph) them where possible.

- Make sure there is no mistreatment of the animals that you see—in some countries animals are exploited for entertainment and money.

- A little research will help you find respected local animal sanctuaries that protect animals. Many of these places rely solely on donations to survive, so if you are taking photographs of the animals there, consider making a donation.

TECHNIQUE

- Look at the wider location and ask if it adds to the overall image. Should you include more of the setting, or should the sign be the sole subject?

- Watch out for reflections from some modern or glass signs.

READ ALL ABOUT IT

Signs make great travel subjects, as they help give your photographs a little more context by revealing to your viewer where you were when you took the image. They are also all around us, providing instructions and information no matter where we are traveling to, so you shouldn't find any shortage of subject matter for this assignment.

Your mission (continued on pages 84–5) is to create a set of images of the different signs that you see around you. Look for signs that are unique in some way and focus on those that contain something distinctive, whether they are serious or humorous, contain strange pictures, or are written in a local language. These signs can really help to add foreign flavor to your travel shots.

PRO TIPS

Neon signs can make a great series of images, but they can be tricky to photograph well. Here are some handy hints:

- Neon is most prominent at night, but you will need to use a wide aperture and a high ISO if you want to handhold your camera. If not, a tripod is ideal.

- Turn off your camera's flash.

- Your camera can easily get confused and underexpose your image as it tries to balance the neon. Make sure that you meter for the whole scene rather than just the brightness of the neon light.

- The closer you get to the sign, the less the background will affect the exposure.

- Set the white balance to Daylight to produce natural and accurate colors.

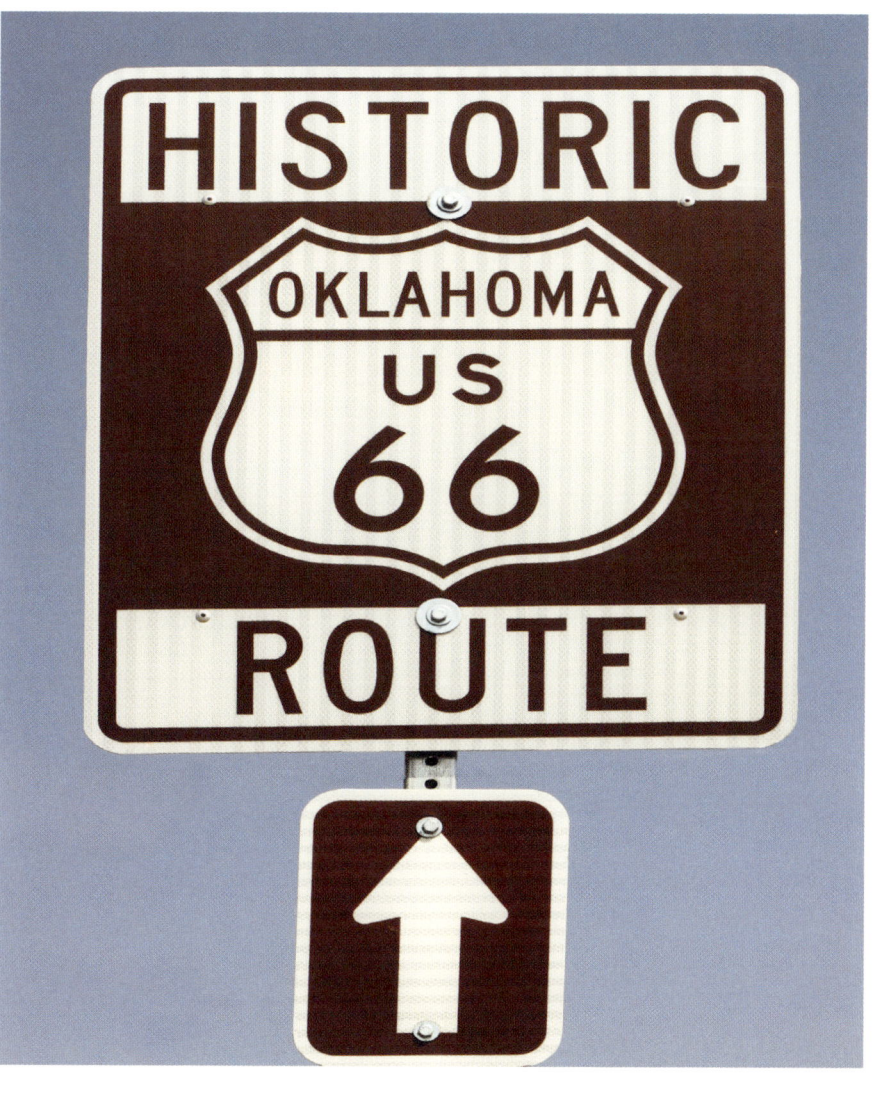

▲ During a road trip in the USA I captured a small selection of the signs that were encountered along the route, which revealed a lot about the areas I was visiting. This informative road sign clearly documents where I was and which highway I was on.

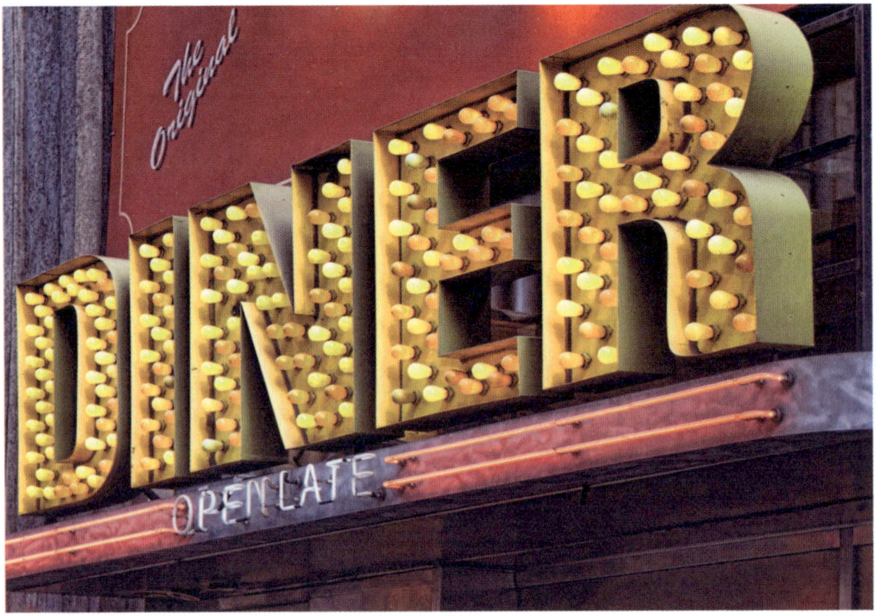

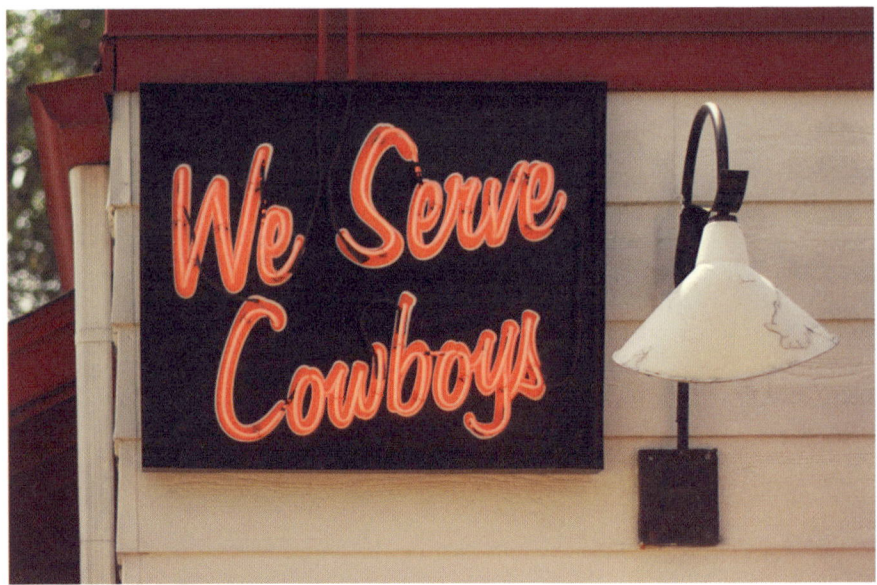

▲ Looking for somewhere to stop for lunch, it was hard to miss this sign with its many lights.

▲ Some signs are clearly unique–this neon one outside a small diner welcomed the local clientele.

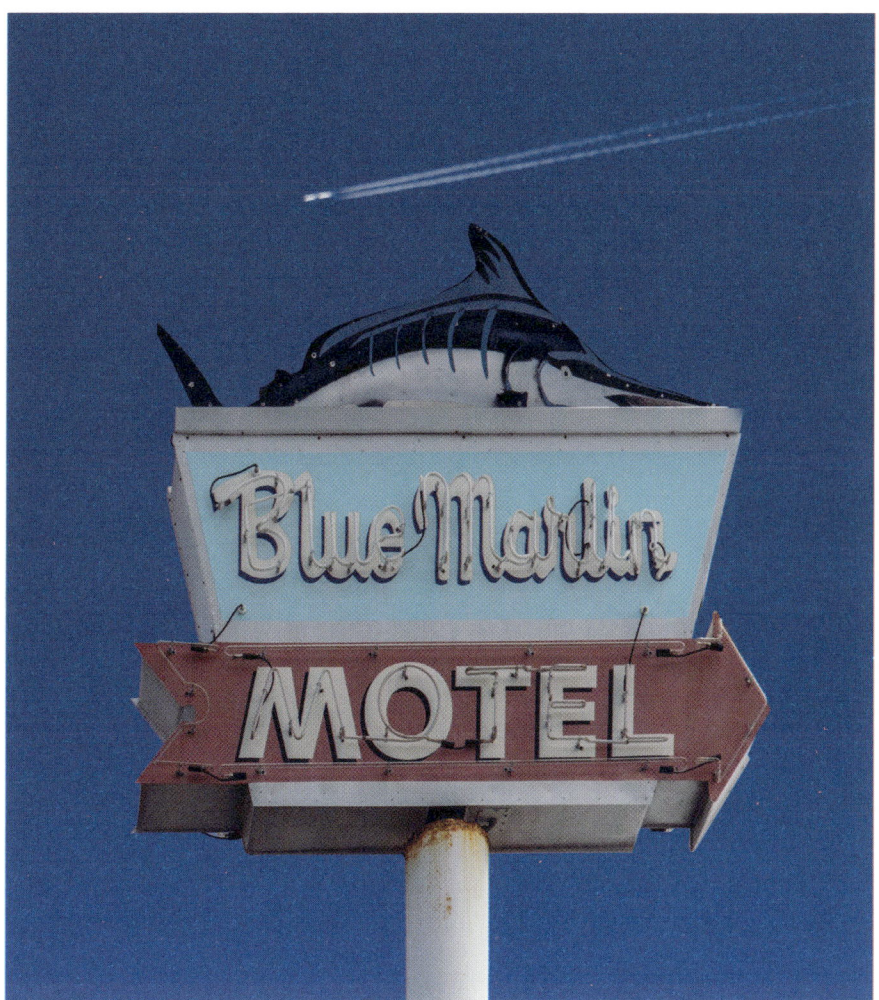

TRAVEL NOTES

- To make your series more coherent you might choose to stick to one distinct type of sign, such as neon signs (see Pro Tips on page 82), advertising and billboards, warning signs, street and road signs, store windows and shop signs, or posters and flyers.

▲ *This vintage sign caught my eye. The vapor trails of the airplane in the distance add another dimension of travel, and create a contrast of old and new.*

TRAVEL NOTES

- Planning ahead can help ease the pressure of traveling. It can also be reassuring to have important information to hand in case of an emergency, especially insurance information.

- A little bit of advance research can avoid wasted time when you arrive. Even something as basic as a list of "must see" and "must photograph" locations will help.

- Consider downloading local maps onto your phone or tablet in advance of your trip.

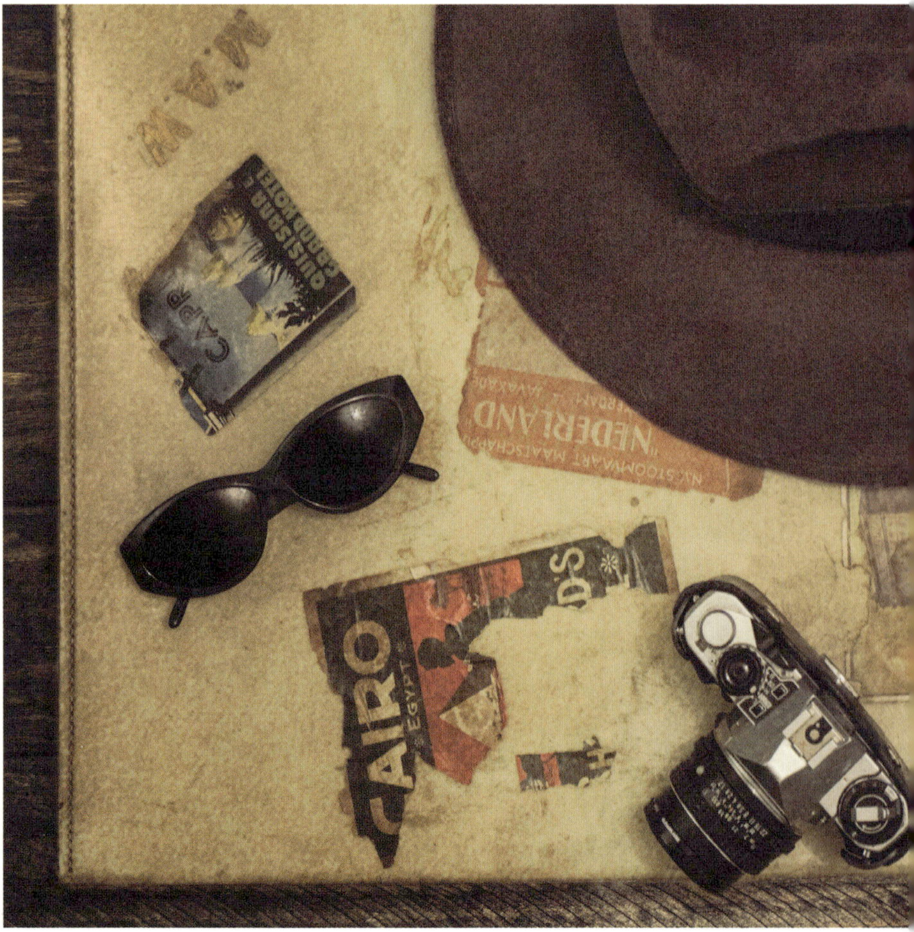

- These images don't have to be staged or posed—a candid capture of the moment can create a photograph that is full of emotion.

- You don't need to photograph people. You could create a strong still life using the documents, maps, brochures, and other reference material for the trip ahead. However, try not to include any confidential or private information if you are going to post the image online.

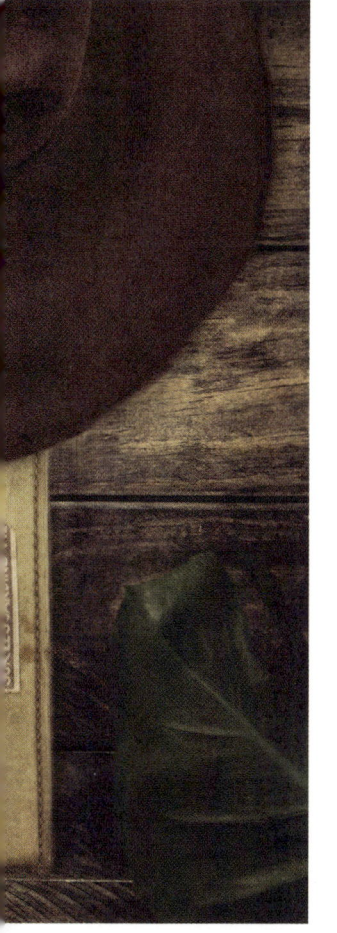

▼ *You might choose to photograph some of the essentials you will be taking with you, such as a suitcase, maps, plans, or tickets that reveal a bit about your journey and your destination.*

MAP IT OUT

There is an important step to take before you embark on your travels: planning and research. A wealth of information is available that can help make any trip more enjoyable and rewarding, and this will usually be accessed long before you've reached your destination.

For this assignment, the aim is to create an image that summarizes the planning stages of a trip. Perhaps you haven't left yet and want to capture the building excitement for your forthcoming adventure, or perhaps you are sitting in a train station, airport lounge, or gas station trying to make a last-minute change to your itinerary.

Either way, use this opportunity to capture the essence of how you and your fellow travelers are feeling. A happy image showing everyone full of anticipation and excitement will make a great shot, but it's a rather obvious choice, so try to shoot something that captures a real-life moment of potential problem-solving, teamwork, and collaboration.

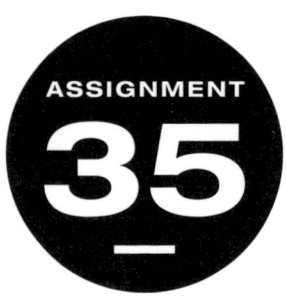

ASSIGNMENT

35

TECHNIQUE

- Your choice of shutter speed is crucial here, with slower shutter speeds exaggerating motion and energy.

- If you can't achieve a slow shutter speed on a bright day consider using a neutral density (ND) filter over the lens.

TRAVEL NOTES

- Choosing the best time to photograph your urban images is vital. The angle of the sun can transform the mood in your images.

- Rain and wind will change the nature of a city. This can be an interesting time to head out and shoot (see Assignment 29).

- Many cities have skyscrapers and other tall structures that offer spectacular views of the streets below, providing a great location to take dramatic images.

- Try to think about the essence of where you are. What makes it special and different to other locations? Try to include this in your images.

- Movement doesn't have to be fast-paced—it can also be reflected in more unique forms of local transportation such as bicycles, rickshaws, or even animals.

PRO TIPS

- Explore the city on foot and look for good vantage points over busy areas, such as road intersections, bridges, or subway and train station exits.

- At night, the trails created by the lights on moving vehicles can add a strong compositional element to your photographs. Your camera will need to be stationary for these longer exposures and a remote release can make it easier to trigger the shutter without knocking the camera.

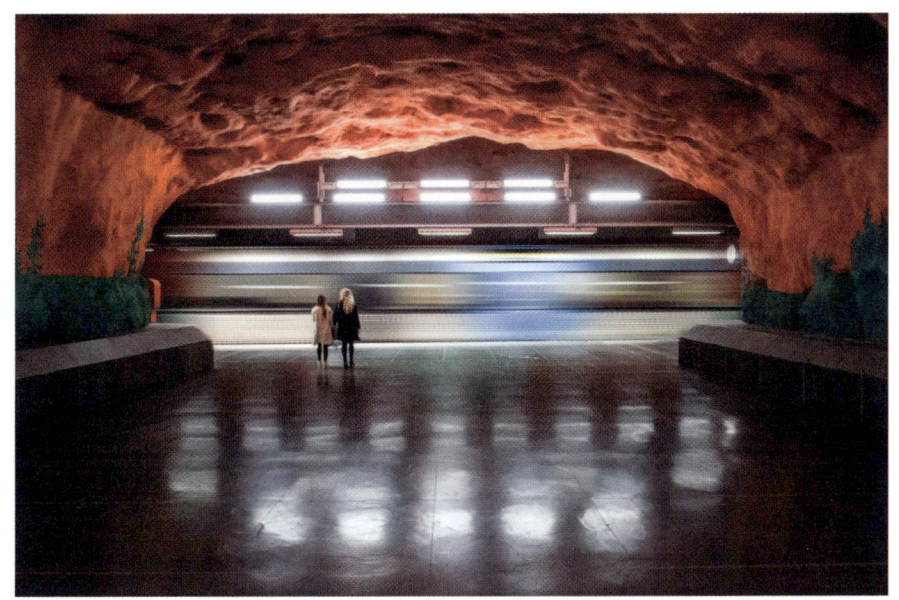

▲ *With my camera on a tripod I was able to capture the blurred movement of a subway train pulling into a station in Stockholm, Sweden. The two people waiting for the train remained stationary long enough to be captured sharply.*

THE SPEED OF THE CITY

City life moves quickly, and the hustle and bustle of traffic and pedestrians heading to and from destinations unknown, together with the sounds and smells, can create a true sense of energy. Being so far removed from the quiet scenic backdrop of the countryside and coast, capturing the movement and activity within cities can create incredibly compelling photographs.

Documenting the essence of metropolitan life is the focus of this assignment. Although this will differ depending on the particular city you are in, you will notice there is a common theme among most urban environments, such as bustling sidewalks, crowded public transport, commuters, bold advertising, noisy construction sites, and more. Start by thinking about which aspects of the urban environment you want to emphasize and how you can really capture the vibrancy of city life.

ASSIGNMENT

36

TECHNIQUE

- Composition is key. You want to make sure your images include the difference between the conflicting elements and show their context.

- Try to reveal a sense of place to give your images extra meaning.

- Think about depth of field and whether you want one of the elements to be implied, by throwing it out of focus, or whether you want a deeper depth of field that gives everything equal prominence.

OPPOSITES ATTRACT

Images that contain a mixture of opposing elements can influence the way your viewers interact with your images, making them think more about what is going on in the scene and what it is you're trying to convey. The aim for this assignment is to look around for a strong contrast between two key elements and capture them within a single image: these can be direct opposites between the subjects or objects, or implied differences.

You may initially find this assignment a little tricky, but once you slow down and start looking you will see that these juxtapositions are much more commonplace than you might originally have thought. If you are still struggling, an easier alternative is to create a diptych, by taking two images in the same area of two opposing subjects and placing them together in postproduction.

ASSIGNMENT JOURNAL

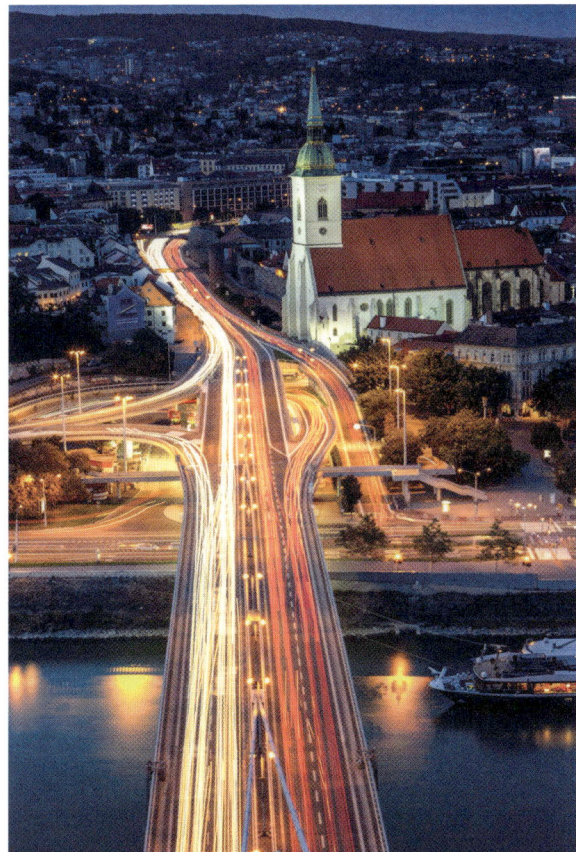

▲ *In this image taken in Bratislava, Slovakia, an old 15th-century cathedral in the city center competes for attention with the modern Danube Bridge, covered with light trails created by the fast-flowing traffic.*

TRAVEL NOTES

Effective juxtapositions could include:

- Old and new

- Modern and traditional

- Light and dark

- Natural and man-made

- Big and small

- Male and female

- Soft and hard

- Strong and weak

- Shapes

- Body language or emotions

- Privilege and poverty

PRO TIPS

- Playing with the position of your subject and its background can be an effective way of reinforcing the juxtaposition.

- Try to keep your images as simple as possible to help emphasize the contrasting elements in the frame. You don't want them to become lost in a complex image with lots of competing details.

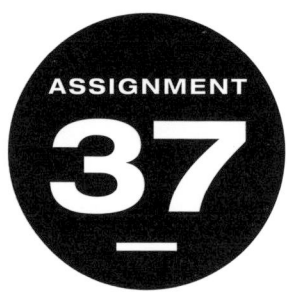

ASSIGNMENT

37

TECHNIQUE

- The paint can often be quite reflective in harsh sunlight, so it can be easier to shoot on cloudy days or when the art is in shade.

- With smaller pieces, including more of the wider location can sometimes create a more interesting image.

- Introducing people or other objects can give an indication of scale, add contrast to a scene, or perhaps even support the story in the graffiti itself.

PRO TIPS

- When processing your street art images, consider boosting the contrast and vibrance to emphasize bold colors.

- Crop your images in postproduction to tighten up the composition.

- A lot of graffiti can help to create a "grungy" look in your images.

TRAVEL NOTES

- It is not particularly hard to locate street art, but bear in mind that the prime urban areas are usually a little away from the popular tourist trail.

- You can search online to find the best spots to visit, but you will often encounter street art while you are walking around and exploring.

- It goes without saying that you should watch out for your personal safety, especially if you are walking around alone with expensive camera gear in a tough neighborhood.

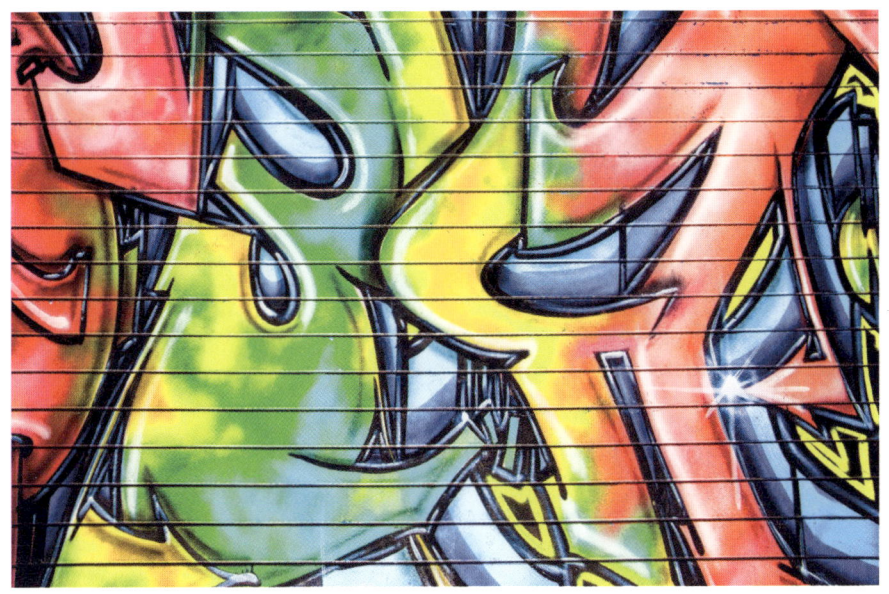

▲ *Look for bold and colorful graffiti if you want to make images that really pop.*

CITY WALLS

Graffiti and street art have become more mainstream in recent years and are a common part of the urban landscape. The art can be a great subject in itself, or form part of a broader cityscape image. It can also provide a backdrop for portraits or show the personality of a neighborhood.

Like most art, street art and graffiti usually has a message behind it that the artist wants to convey. Look out for messages that are clear and understandable and relate to the area or country that you are visiting. They can provide a really interesting opportunity to document a political or social issue, or add a topical and vibrant local community statement to an image.

Your assignment here is to capture the essence of a place by including some street art within your images. The art can be the main subject or part of a bigger scene, but you should set out to capture a piece of street art or graffiti that is not only attractive, but also reveals a little bit of the character of your travel destination.

ASSIGNMENT

38

TECHNIQUE

- Don't just capture snapshots, but think about a balance of foreground, background, and points of interest. Composition is still important.

- Carry the minimum amount of equipment. A camera with a zoom lens might be all you need.

- If it is dark, or the light is not so strong, increase your ISO rather than extending your shutter speed—you don't want to start introducing camera shake.

MYSTERY TOUR

Exploring somewhere new on your travels is naturally very exciting and you really don't know what you'll end up seeing and what encounters you'll have. Discovering new sights, people, and places is the essence of traveling well, and when it comes to your photography there is something to be said for packing light and wandering around a new destination to learn more about your new surroundings.

Your assignment here is to do just that. There is no real mission or preconceived image list: just get out there, explore, and capture at least 15 images of anything and everything that you discover. Try to get off the beaten track and away from the usual tourist trails and immerse yourself in the areas where locals congregate. As you wander around, choose random streets to walk down, peer into buildings and doorways, and look for interesting photographic opportunities.

Consider taking a bus or other public transport to an unknown destination—this can allow you to see more diverse areas and get an insight into how the locals live. Deliberately getting lost can reveal some of the lesser-known parts of a particular place and enable you to uncover some photographic gems. You'll also get to see more than the average tourist!

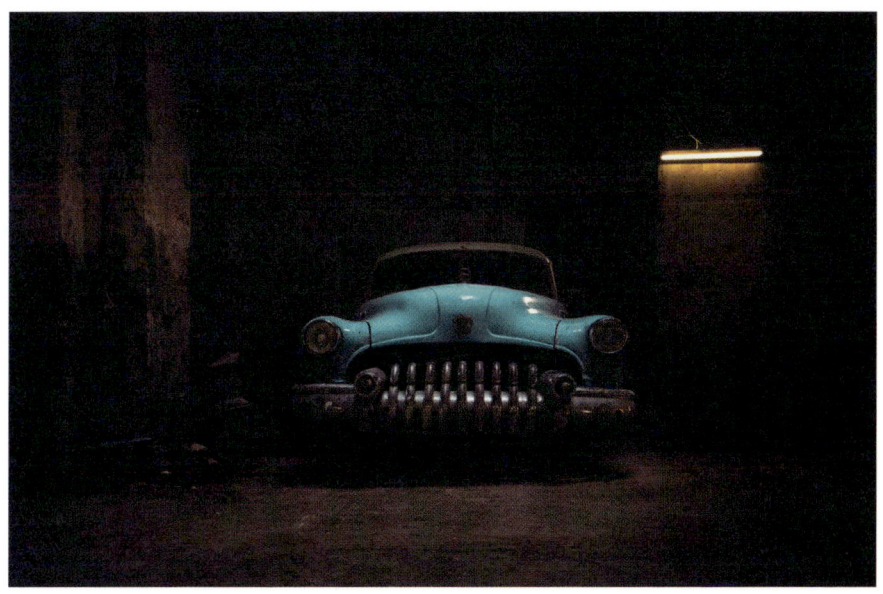

▲ *Exploring new places is part of the adventure. I stumbled on this car-parking garage while wandering down some quiet side streets in Havana, Cuba.*

PRO TIPS

- If you are out in bright sunshine, a lens hood and a polarizing filter can help reduce glare.

- Try to blend in, rather than standing out as an obvious photographer.

- Decide on your favorite photograph and print it when you return home.

TRAVEL NOTES

- Take care when wandering, especially if you are exploring off the beaten track. Trust your instincts!

- Respect people's privacy and personal space. Seek permission before you walk into somewhere that may be private.

- It can be a good idea to ask a friendly local for advice about any areas that are worth exploring, as well as places that should be avoided.

ASSIGNMENT

39

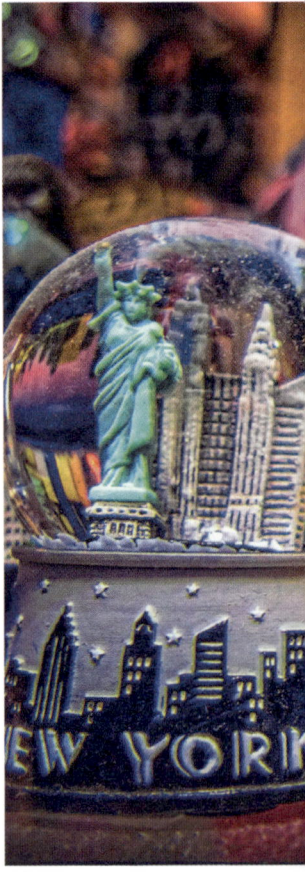

PRO TIPS

- If you are going to photograph in a shop, ask the owner for permission.

- You might choose to include shoppers and create an environmental portrait, or hone in on the items to produce a kitsch still life.

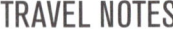

TRAVEL NOTES

- Replicas of the main landmarks and attractions of the area you are visiting will reveal a little more about your location. You might also consider buying one to photograph in front of the real thing (see Assignment 21).

- Sometimes the language printed on T-shirts, clothing, and posters can be misspelled or misconstrued, which can add humor to an image.

TECHNIQUE

- Backgrounds can often be cluttered, so consider visually "decluttering" your shots by using a wide aperture to blur the background or by filling the frame with your chosen subject.

- Look for strong and vivid colors, and repeat patterns created by rows of similar items.

- Obtaining an accurate white balance can be tricky, so shoot Raw and set the white balance during postproduction.

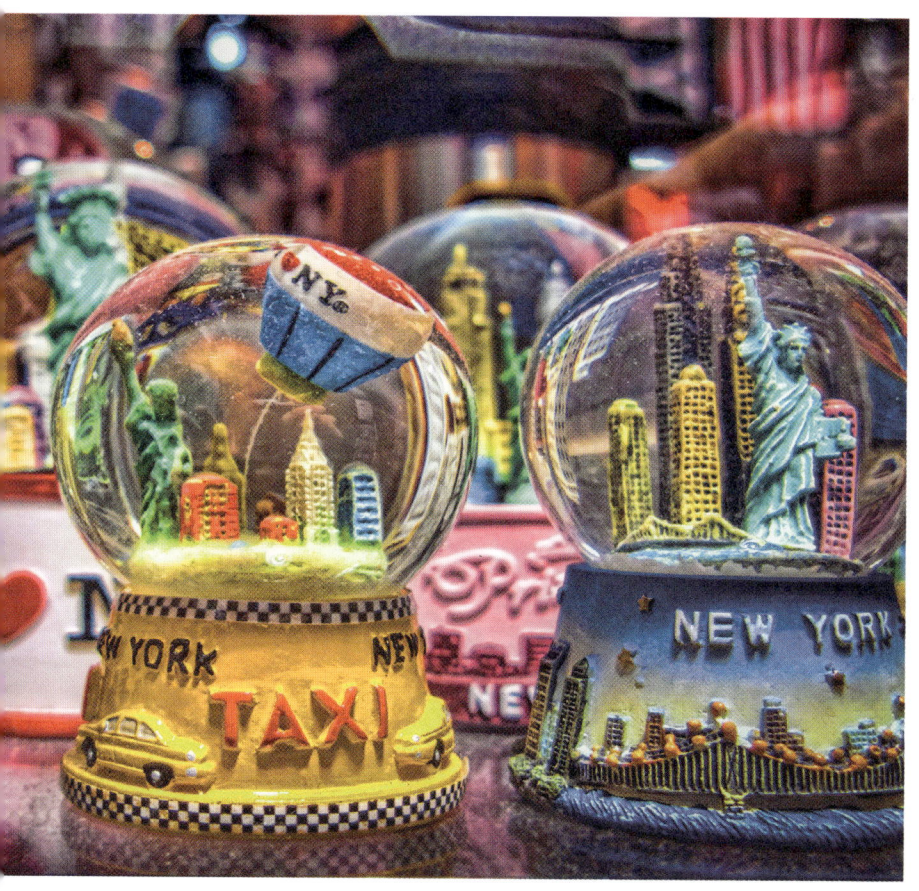

▲ *This collection of snowglobes on a tourist shop shelf was crying out to be photographed, so I zoomed in close to fill the frame.*

KITSCH IS COOL

Wherever you are headed, you will pass tourist shops full of cheap plastic toys, fridge magnets, and other local mementos. Although a plastic replica of a majestic building or landmark might seem vulgar to some, these cheap souvenirs can make a fun subject. So what better way to document where you are, than to wander through these Aladdin's caves of kitsch and capture some interesting photographs of the treasures inside?

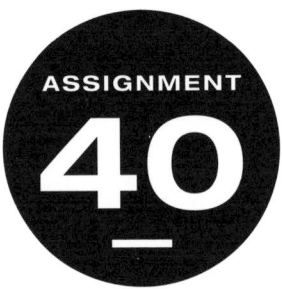

TECHNIQUE

- Set your camera to its monochrome shooting mode and shoot Raw and JPEG images simultaneously. This will give you a black-and-white playback image on the camera screen (the JPEG file), which will help you visualize the scene in monochrome. You can then convert the Raw file to black and white in postproduction to retain the highest image quality.

▼ *The harsh midday sun is usually unforgiving for photography. Here, a clear blue sky didn't add to the image so I chose to convert this shot of the Eiffel Tower in Paris to black and white, and darken the sky right down. The low angle of view adds to the graphic nature of the shot.*

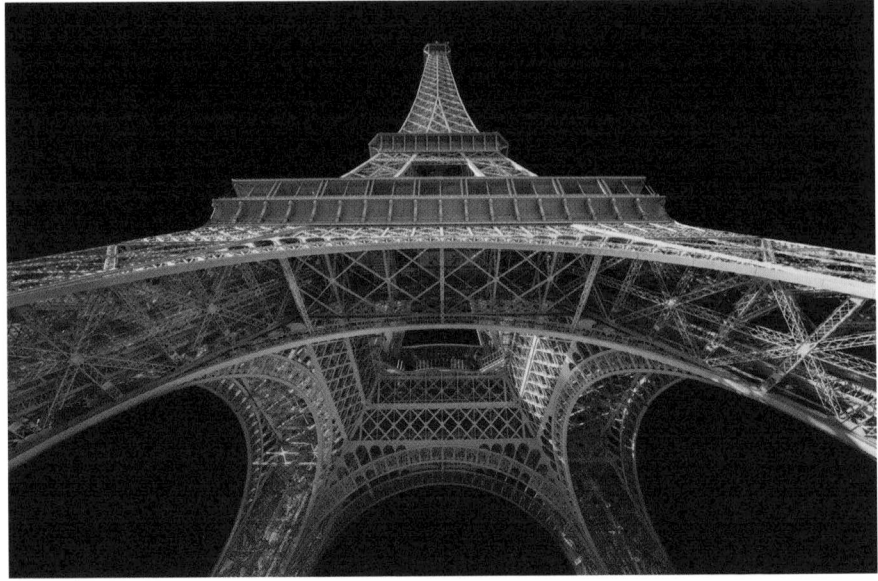

MONOTONE MEMORIES

There is a tendency to capture travel images in color, as this is the "true" representation of what we see with our eyes. Sometimes, stripping the color from a scene can help to simplify a photograph, enabling the audience to better understand where you were and why you took the shot. Black-and-white images can also be more expressive, with heightened emotion.

Your assignment is to create and print a set of strong black-and-white images that tell a compelling visual story. You will need to choose you subject matter carefully, and think in black and white, as simply removing the color from your shots will not necessarily create the strongest monotone photographs.

Think about the contrast between the elements in your shot and how colors will translate to shades of gray—red and green, for example, can look identical when they're converted to black and white. Look at shapes and textures, and how variations in tone can help you create something visually captivating. Playing with darker backgrounds and brighter subjects can really help you to focus the viewer's attention where you want it.

PRO TIPS

- Consider shooting when the light is harsh and strong—intense light and dark shadows translate well into black and white.

- Avoid scenes with low contrast, as these tend not to work well in black and white.

- Minimalist images can work well in black and white (see Assignment 41).

TRAVEL NOTES

- Monochrome images can heighten the mood of a shot, so consider what you are trying to say with your image and let this guide your decision to convert a photograph to black and white.

- Black and white can simplify a scene, as well as emphasizing lines, textures, and patterns, so it pays to look for strong, graphic subjects.

TECHNIQUE

- The placement and size of your subject is important. Give it enough "breathing room" so that it has space to sit and draw your viewers' attention. Think about how you can use your shooting position and focal length to isolate the subject, but still have sufficient space around it—this negative space is one of the most important elements in your minimalist shot.

- Make your subject stand out through your use of color, contrast, shape, light, pattern, shadow, or brightness.

- A wide aperture will throw the background out of focus, which can minimize any distractions and make your subject "pop."

TRAVEL NOTES

- Your subject should really capture the essence of where you are—this should not be a purely abstract image.

- Nature can provide strong elements for this type of minimal photography, such as a lone tree or animal against a stark or plain background.

PRO TIPS

- Harmonious color combinations—where your subject is a similar color to the background—can often work well, but also consider using complementary color schemes, where your subject contrasts with its background.

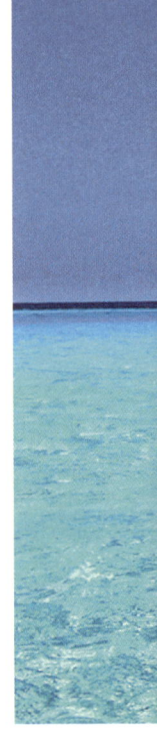

▶ *"Balance" and "visual weight" are compositional terms used to describe how different elements sit in the frame and relate to one another. In this shot the lone cloud balances with the large expanse of water. Despite their difference in size, they both have the same visual weight.*

KEEP IT SIMPLE

Arriving somewhere new can often be overwhelming. What should you focus on and photograph? How should you compose your shots and what should you include when there's so much going on? These questions are quite common, and for this assignment the answer is straightforward: "keep it simple."

The idea here is to strip back the scene and create a minimal shot, so choose one strong and compelling element and make it the sole emphasis of your composition. This doesn't mean simply zooming in so it fills the frame, but the exact opposite. Try to frame your subject in a way that includes plenty of "negative" space, so the remainder of the shot is quite stark, without any elements vying for your audience's attention. You can achieve this by limiting the use of bold colors, or searching for simple, clutter-free backgrounds.

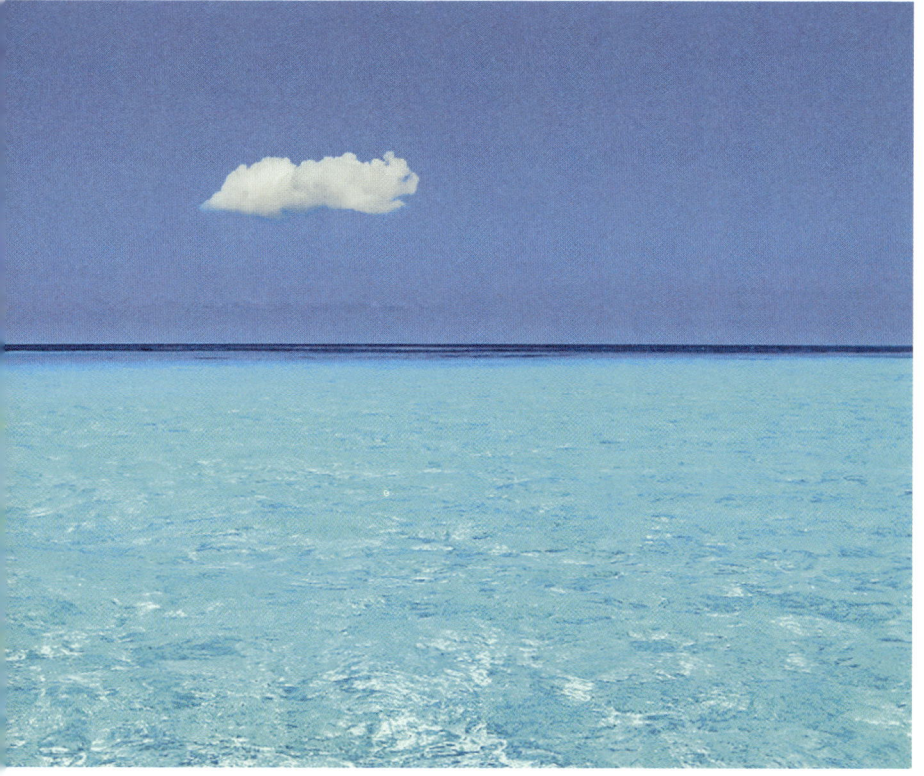

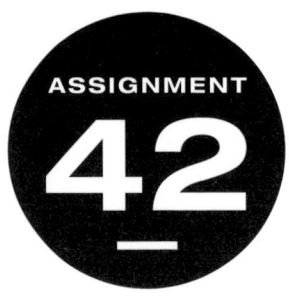

ASSIGNMENT

42

TECHNIQUE

- Try not to rush or feel pressured to just snap away. You've taken time to travel to a particular location, so take a moment to soak it all in before you start shooting.

- Lighting is important, and the best light will usually be during the golden hour that follows sunrise and is just before sunset.

- If your only option is to shoot at midday or with harsh light, consider converting your shots to black and white to make the most of strong contrast (see Assignment 40).

- If the sky is flat and boring—perhaps solid gray cloud—consider framing your image to avoid including too much of it or exclude it entirely from your shot.

PRO TIPS

- Check the weather forecast and see if there is a day that promises particularly good weather conditions that you can capitalize on for your photography.

- Avoid the biggest crowds that will inevitably assemble at popular travel destinations by getting to your chosen location early or staying late.

- Speak to locals and don't be afraid to ask for photographic advice—you may end up discovering locations that you weren't aware of.

TRAVEL NOTES

- Research is key. Check to see what famous views, landmarks, and other structures your location is famous for—you don't want to return home without that iconic shot.

- Consider booking a room with a view. Being close to (or possibly even overlooking) something you want to photograph can give you some fairly unique opportunities.

- Shooting the skyline is a great option for city visits. Check out existing postcards in local stores to give you inspiration and ideas for locations to shoot from.

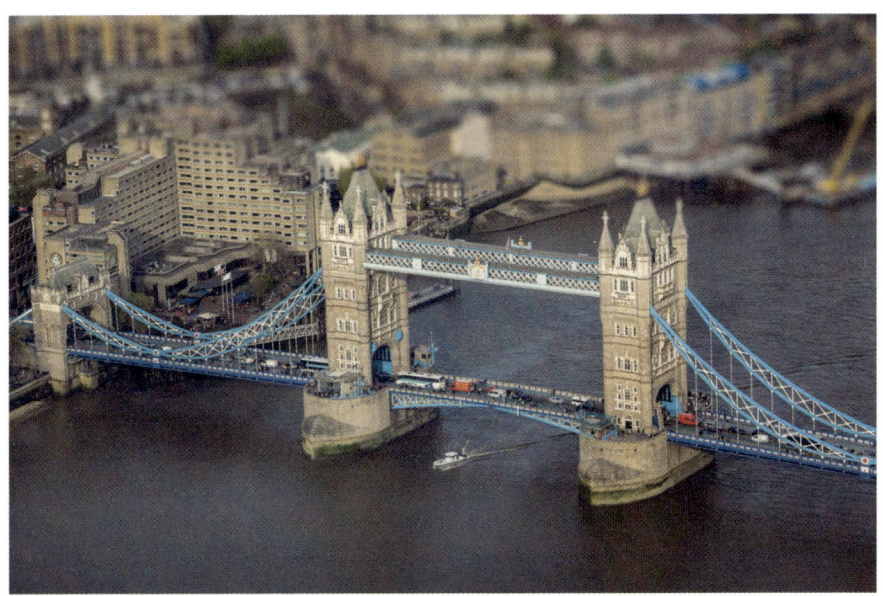

▲ *A high viewpoint can provide a great opportunity to obtain strong postcard images of landmarks in their entirety. Here a "tilt-shift" effect makes London's Tower Bridge look like a small toy.*

PICTURE POSTCARD

It is only natural that you will want to visit the famous landmarks in the place you are traveling in. Whether they are man-made or natural, they are likely to be impressive sites, but are usually very busy. They will also have been photographed by thousands of tourists before you, and often from the same or similar angle, but that doesn't mean you shouldn't photograph them as well.

Photographing the traditional angles that are regularly seen is a good way of creating images that your audience will be expecting to see. These are also the angles that capture the site at its best, which is why so many people photograph them from the same spot.

The aim of this assignment is to take a classic "picture postcard" shot of the most famous landmark in your location. You will need to research the best shooting locations and angles, the best time of day (or night), and maybe find some examples of strong images that other people have already shot to inspire you.

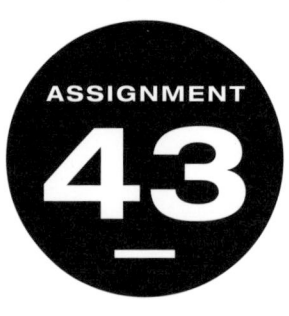

ASSIGNMENT

43

TECHNIQUE

- Composition is always important. Decide where to place people in an image, paying particular attention to the background.

- Increasing your exposure by ½ stop can help produce a brighter image, but take care in bright conditions not to overexpose your photograph.

- Always focus on your subject's eyes.

- Try to avoid positioning your subject so they are facing the sun, as this will cause them to squint.

PRO TIPS

- A smile goes a long way and helps break down any language barriers. It can also make your subject feel more at ease.

- Don't forget to focus on the details of your subject's outfit, as specific aspects of their clothing can often reveal more of their story.

- Decide whether you want to take a candid image of a person without directing them to pose, or whether you want to ask permission first and take a more formal shot. Both approaches will offer different results.

TRAVEL NOTES

- Always be respectful. Your desired subject is not dressing for you and may not want to be photographed.

- Don't just snap and run. Show your subject the image you have taken and perhaps offer to send them a copy.

- Find out a little about the culture and its people, as this will help you judge when or how to take images.

- Sometimes people will request payment in exchange for their images, so you may want to have some money ready to give if you feel it is appropriate. However, in some cultures it is considered offensive to offer money, so it pays to check the local customs.

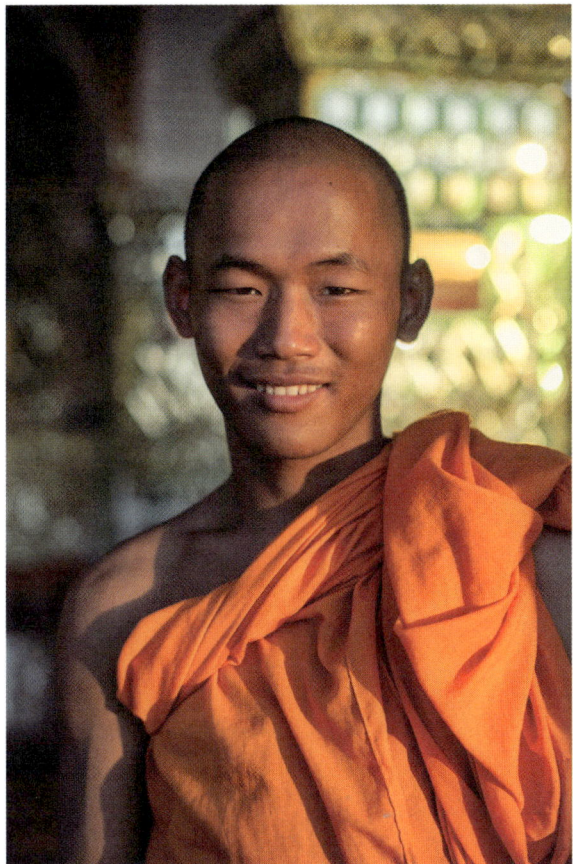

◀ *The bright sunlight emphasizes the orange robe of this trainee monk and also highlights the golden metal of the temple behind him. A wide aperture was used to throw the background out of focus.*

SUITS TO SAREES

Travel photography portraits are often strongest when they connect the subject and their culture, and traditional dress is a great way of showing this. Traditional dress can be incredibly wide ranging, and can include adornments such as crystals and flower garlands, brightly dyed robes and shawls, and intricate, hand-stitched outfits emblazoned with beadwork that reveals traditional stories and folklore.

Photographing a local person in their traditional clothing is your assignment here. Depending where you are, this may just mean including something as simple as a local hat or head wrap, or a mixture of modern clothing with elements of more old-fashioned styles. Try to focus on what the clothing tells the viewer about your subject—who they are, their status, their culture—as well as the beauty or unusual nature of the design, or other aspects of the local fashion.

ASSIGNMENT 44

TECHNIQUE

- The standard focal length is very versatile and with a little practice you will find that it is not too wide, nor too long, and creates images with very little distortion.

- Be selective with your compositions. Play with your angles and perspective to find and frame interesting shots.

- Try to fill the frame with interesting elements or negative space. If things look too far away, take a few steps closer!

▶ *This assignment will force you to be braver when taking images of people, as you will have to get close and engage—you won't be able to hide away and zoom in from a distance. However, this can make your portraits more appealing, as you will be able to talk with your subject and capture them in a more intimate way.*

MOVE YOUR FEET

Lenses fall into two categories: prime lenses with a single, fixed focal length, or zoom lenses that offer a range of focal lengths. The flexibility of a zoom lens is great when you can't get close to your subject, but it can cause you to become a little lazy, standing firmly in one spot and zooming in and out to take your shots.

The idea for this assignment is to take a set of three photographs using the focal length that most closely matches our eye's perspective. This is known as the "standard" focal length and is roughly 50mm on a full-frame camera, 35mm on a camera with an APS-C-sized sensor, and 25mm on a Micro Four Thirds camera. Don't worry if you don't have a prime lens that matches this focal length—just set your zoom lens accordingly and resist the temptation to change the focal length.

With a fixed focal length you will have to compose your shots by moving closer to fill the frame, or further away when you want to add more context to the image. You'll literally be "zooming with your feet," which will make you think harder about what you are photographing.

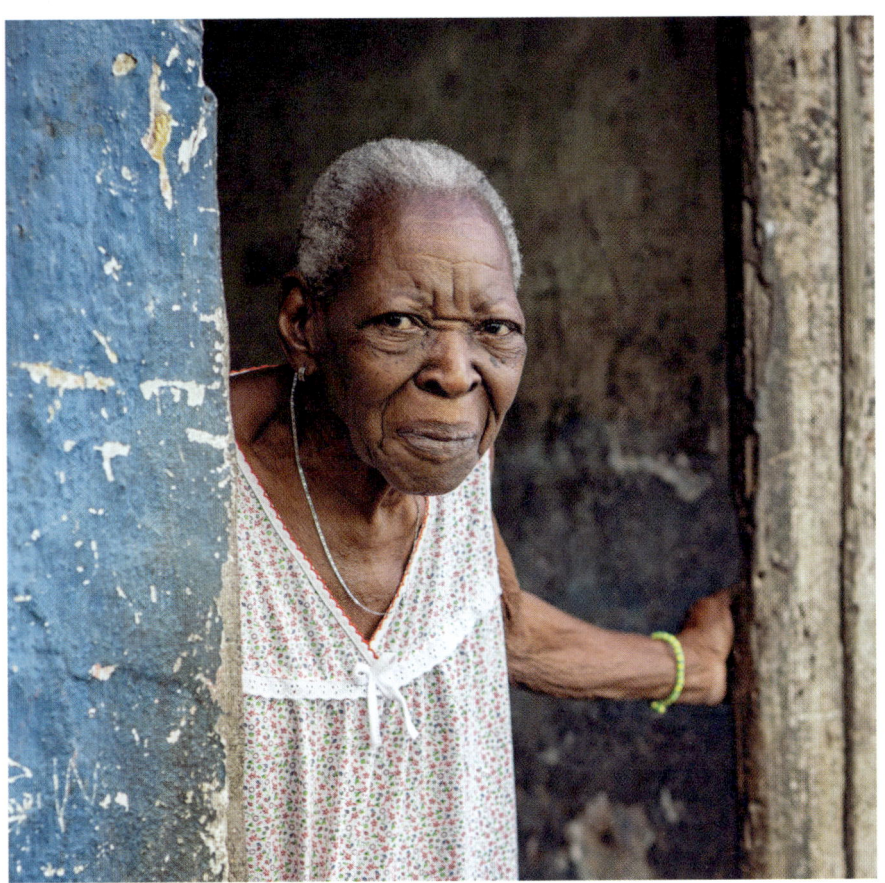

PRO TIPS

- When you get closer to your subject you will often see different and more interesting angles, as you can walk around him or her. If you zoom in from a distance the angles won't necessarily change as much.

- All manufacturers make standard prime lenses and these are often light, inexpensive, and have a wider maximum aperture (typically f/1.8 or f/1.4) than a "standard" zoom lens. This makes them a great walk-around travel lens.

TRAVEL NOTES

- As you may have to get in closer to use a standard lens, take care when shooting certain subjects: if you are taking images of wild animals or a busy street fair, celebration, or protest, for example.

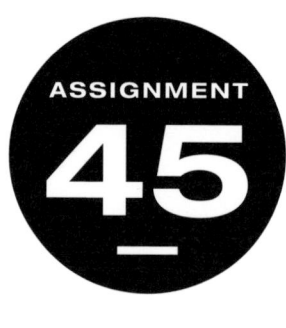

ASSIGNMENT

45

TRAVEL TEXTURES

You will inevitably encounter a multitude of textures on your explorations, which can evoke a sense of place within your images, be it the rough wood and stone of an ancient building or the sleek metal and glass in a modern business district.

However, it can be quite difficult to convey a sense of how something feels in a photograph, but that is your challenge for this assignment: to find textures in your environment that tell the story of the place you're traveling in, and to try to capture that in your image. Rough or smooth, soft or hard, flat or glossy, it really doesn't matter what the texture is, as long as it is interesting and has visual impact.

The textures you are photographing are likely to be interesting details, so look closely all around. It could be the tiny patterns on the back of a leaf, shards of cracked glass, peeling paint, wrinkled skin, the sheen on velvet clothes, or a rusted metal grill on a window—the more you look, the more aware you will become of the range of different textures around you.

ASSIGNMENT JOURNAL

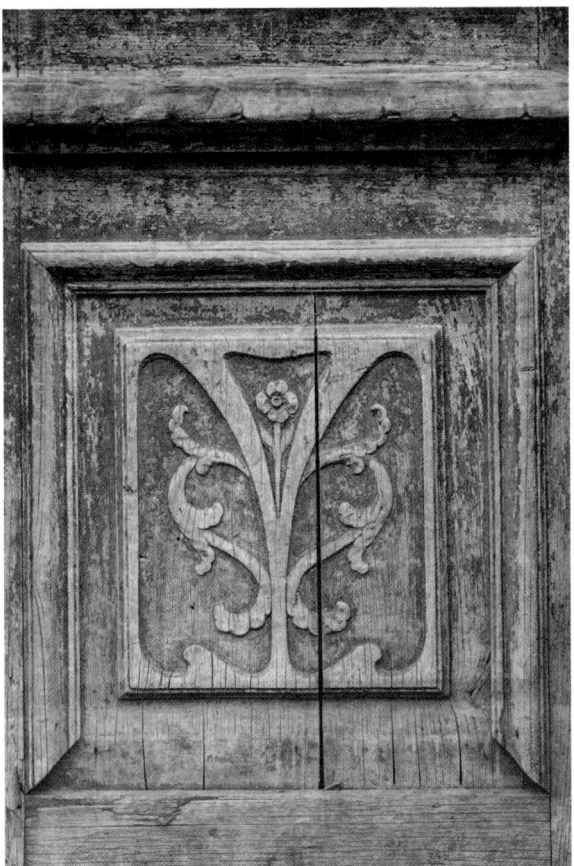

◀ *It was hard to tell what element drew me most to this subject: the intricate carving, the cracked wood, or the faded paint. But they combine to create an image where you can almost feel the wooden surface, just by looking at it.*

TRAVEL NOTES

- Native plants and trees can give a real sense of foreign places. Botanical gardens are often great places to visit when traveling.

- Depending where you are, local construction and architecture will provide a wealth of different textures, ranging from diverse building materials to decaying buildings.

- Local markets will contain a varied supply of textural elements to be photographed, such as food, fabrics, local crafts, and other items. Shoot here and you will find you have an almost endless supply of great subjects.

PRO TIPS

- Not every texture will make an interesting subject. There has to be something else to transform it into a compelling image.

- There needs to be depth to create shadows, and these will help to emphasize the structure and texture of your subject.

- Look for elements that bring your subject to life and give the sense that you can almost feel the texture.

ASSIGNMENT

46

TECHNIQUE

- Slow down and think about why you are taking the photograph and what it reveals to your audience.

- Survey your scene and look for interesting angles and compositions.

- Consider including a human element to make a more relatable article.

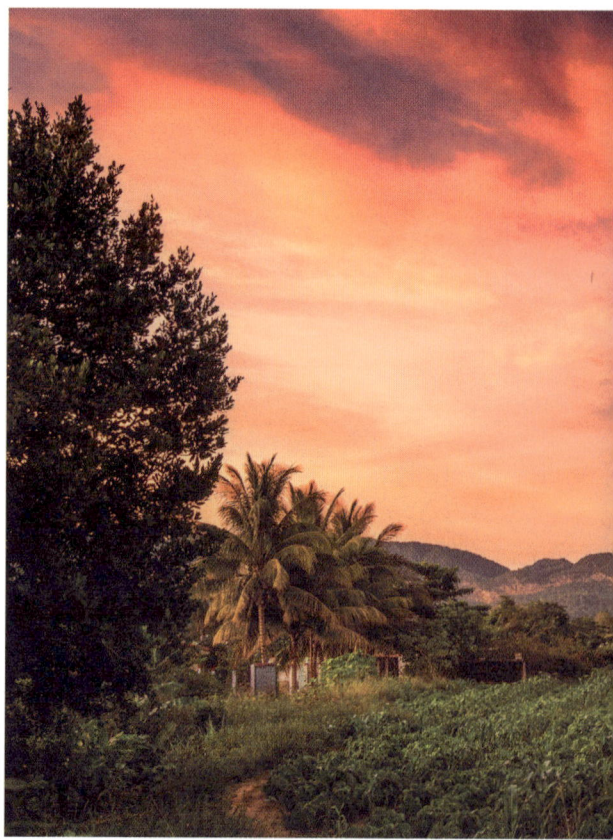

TRAVEL JOURNALIST

Whether they are in magazines or online, travel articles are designed to inspire readers to want to visit far-flung places. The combination of a curated selection of images of beautiful and exciting sights that are all linked to a specific place can really spark the emotions of an audience.

Your assignment (continued on pages 112–13) is to spend the day as a travel journalist, compiling a small selection of eight to ten images that reveal the most intriguing aspects of your location. Decide whether the story will be based on an issue relevant to that particular place, such as pollution or a cultural or social divide, or a more general story about what to see and do in a town, city, or resort. The idea is to think about what you want to include in your collection as you have limited images that you can "submit." Carefully consider what you want to focus on and why, and ask yourself what story each image will tell and how they work together.

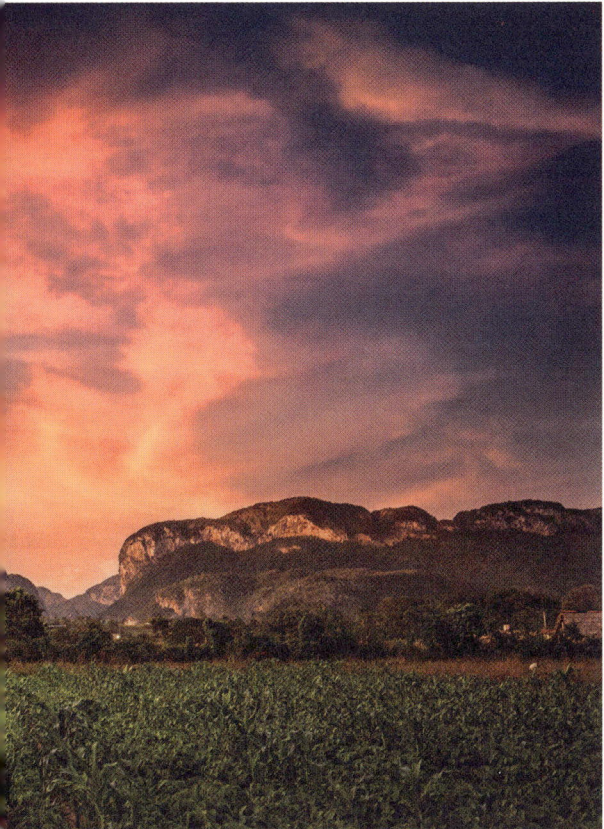

Try to include a wide range of images, from environmental shots that show the landscape and set the scene, to details that reveal what makes the place special and unique. You might also want to try to include some portraits to show the locals who call it home and add a human angle to your story. Take more images than you think you'll need, and then spend time editing them into a strong and cohesive final set.

◄► *Here and on pages 112–13, "Somos Cuba" (We Are Cuba) is a collection of photographs of the Cuban people and landscape. This shot (left) shows a sunset over the tobacco fields.*

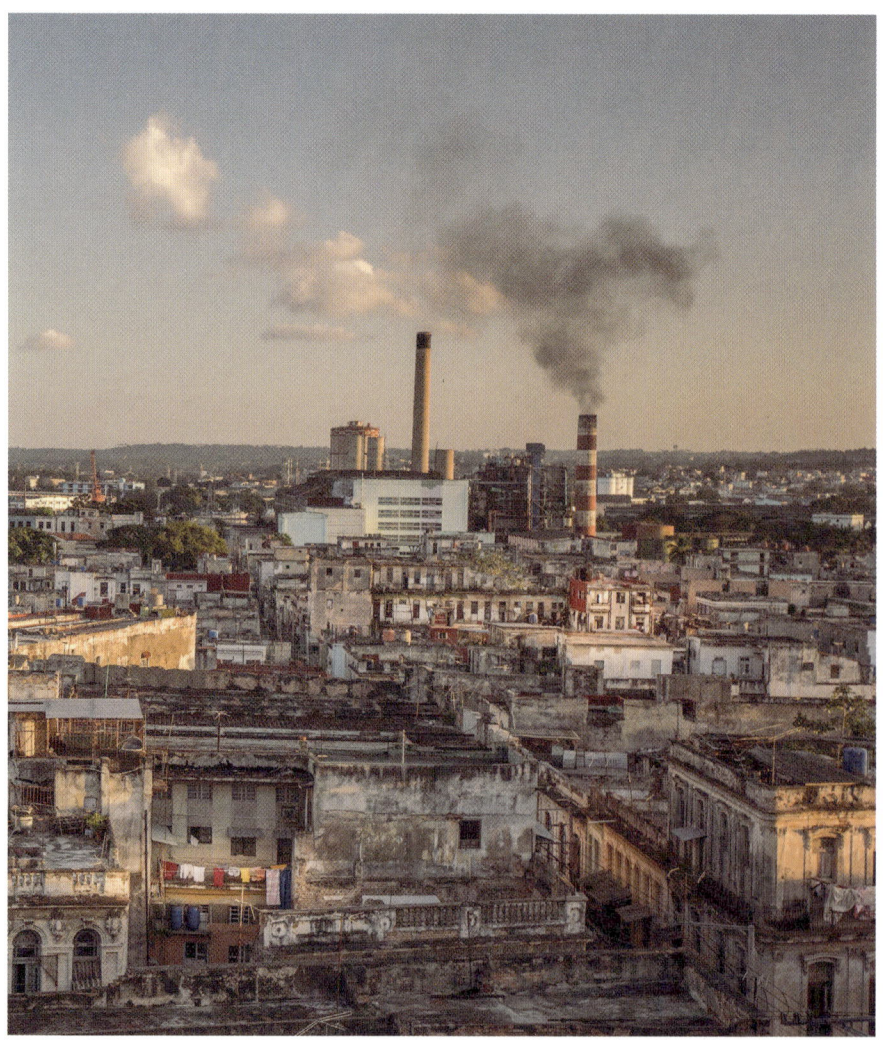

▲ *Old Havana tenements and power station.*

PRO TIPS

- Be selective with the images you include in your final set—if you're not sure about a shot, leave it out.

- Don't include images that don't work with the others in your set or fail to tell the story of your location.

- Use different focal lengths to achieve a range of compositions.

- Mix up the format of your images so you include both landscape (horizontal) and portrait (vertical) format shots.

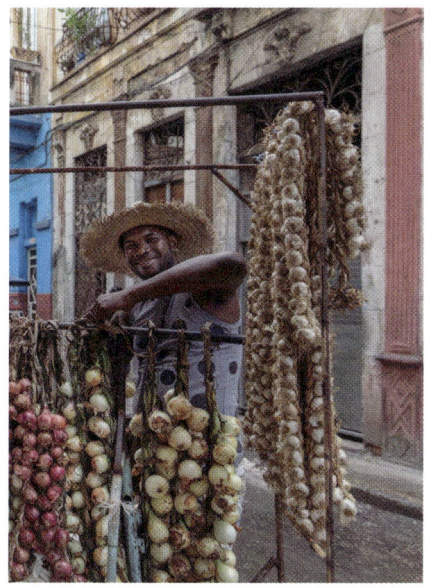

▲ *Jorge the garlic and onion seller.*

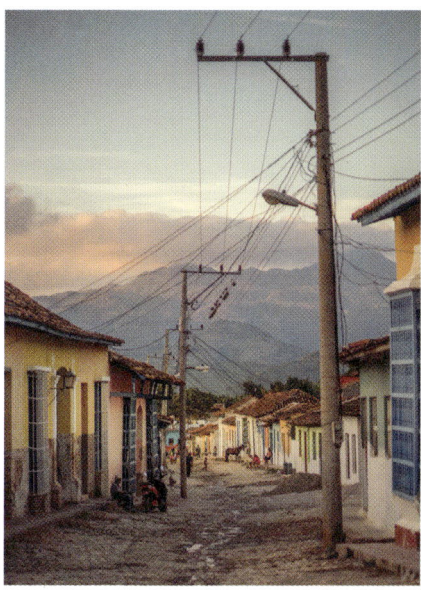

▲ *Street view in the Cuban town of Trinidad.*

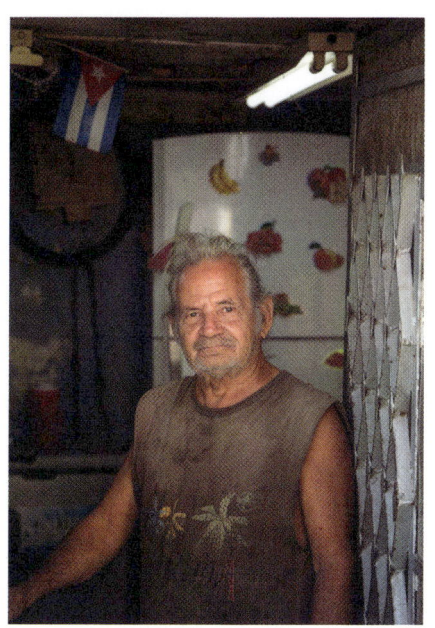

▲ *José the mechanic.*

TRAVEL NOTES

- Think about why you chose to visit this particular destination and what you think will appeal to your viewers.

- Try to capture the ambience of the area. Wander, explore, and observe your new surroundings before you start shooting.

- Always have your camera with you. You never know what you'll see, but being ready will improve your chances of capturing an amazing image.

- Having a basic visual story in mind will help you find and make the images that you want to tell your story, but don't stick to it too rigidly—allow serendipity to play a part as well.

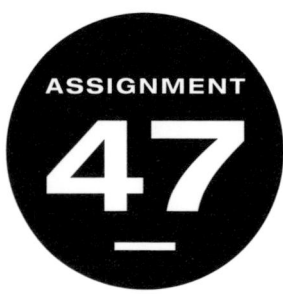

TECHNIQUE

- Documentary-style photography can be tricky, as you will not have much control over the scene. The lighting can often be harsh and other distracting elements can be in your frame.

- Natural, unposed images work best.

▶ *This image captures a woman intensely reading a journal while at work in a beautiful old-fashioned pharmacy. The walls are adorned with a multitude of jars of herbs and potions, while the long wooden counter and interior decorations allude to a time gone by.*

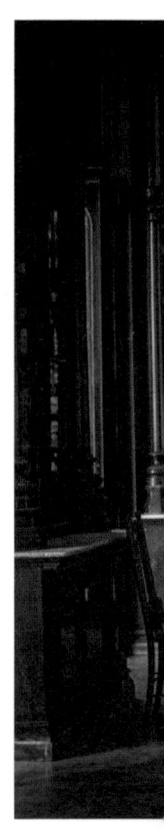

PRO TIPS

- Think about your composition and consider how much of the subject's surroundings you want to reveal to your viewer.

- You may find that you want to keep your distance and use a telephoto lens, or you may prefer to use a wideangle focal length and include more of the scene.

TRAVEL NOTES

- Go to places where people are going about their everyday life.

- Try not to intrude and distract workers for too long.

- Approach people with a smile and with confidence.

- Think about safety if you are in a working environment.

- Take care not to work in forbidden areas or to photograph workers such as immigration officials or soldiers without permission.

ALL IN A DAY'S WORK

Taking portraits of people while they are at work, recording what they do on a daily basis, can help you capture the local character of the area you are visiting. It can also be a powerful way to create travel images that tell a story and are full of intrigue. Including elements of the worker's environment will produce a more compelling and thought-provoking image, which allows the viewer to see more of the subject's character, as well as the reality of their workplace.

Your assignment is to portray the essence of a local worker through their work environment, their execution of a specific job or task, their work uniform or clothes, or a combination of all these elements. Try to consider how the viewer will interpret and understand your image, and whether they will be able to tell what the subject is doing and why. Select one image for printing that you feel conveys the story of the worker and their locale.

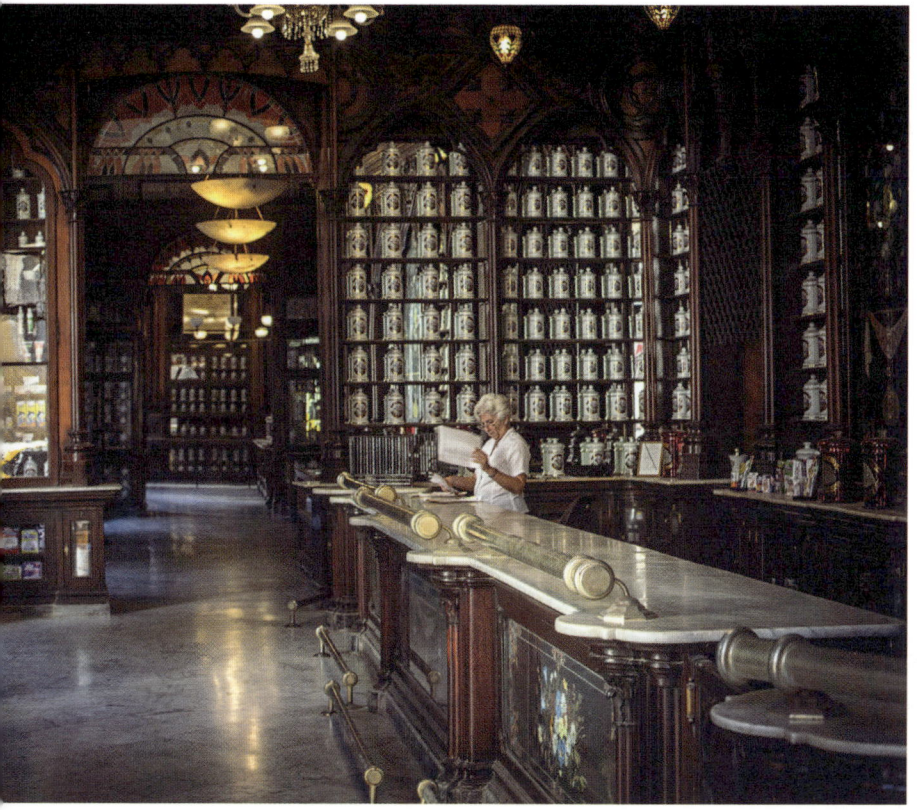

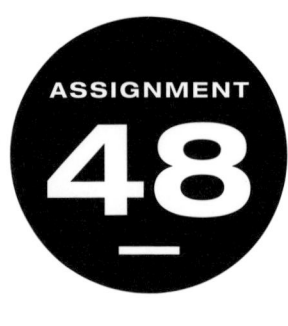

ASSIGNMENT

48

TECHNIQUE

- Old interiors can create difficult exposure challenges, as there is sometimes a wide dynamic range, from bright windows to dark, unlit shadows.

- A tripod or other stable surface can be useful for combating low-light conditions or you can increase the ISO if you're shooting handheld.

- Wideangle lenses can help you capture a sense of emptiness and destruction.

- Look for interesting angles and details. Decide whether the surroundings give the structure any context or add interest.

AMID THE RUINS

Whether it's an old shepherd's hut, an abandoned church, or a deserted industrial building, you are likely to come across derelict architecture in varying states of ruin no matter where you travel. This can sometimes be due to age, neglect, or even extreme weather like hurricanes and earthquakes, but perhaps more commonly you will encounter historical sites. These remnants of ancient civilizations will often have been affected by time and the elements, and appear to be far from their former glory.

There is something incredibly compelling about photographs of places that have fallen into disrepair. They immediately summon stories of the past, making our minds wander and imagine what happened and why, and how they were left to wither away.

The aim of this assignment is to find beauty in the wrecks and remains of something leftover from long-ago or well past its prime. Think about what the subject represents now and how thought-provoking your image will be to your audience. Try to include elements that help tell the story of the place and reveal a little more about how and why it has fallen into decline, whether this was the fall of a civilization, war, abandonment, neglect, or simply nature reclaiming the area.

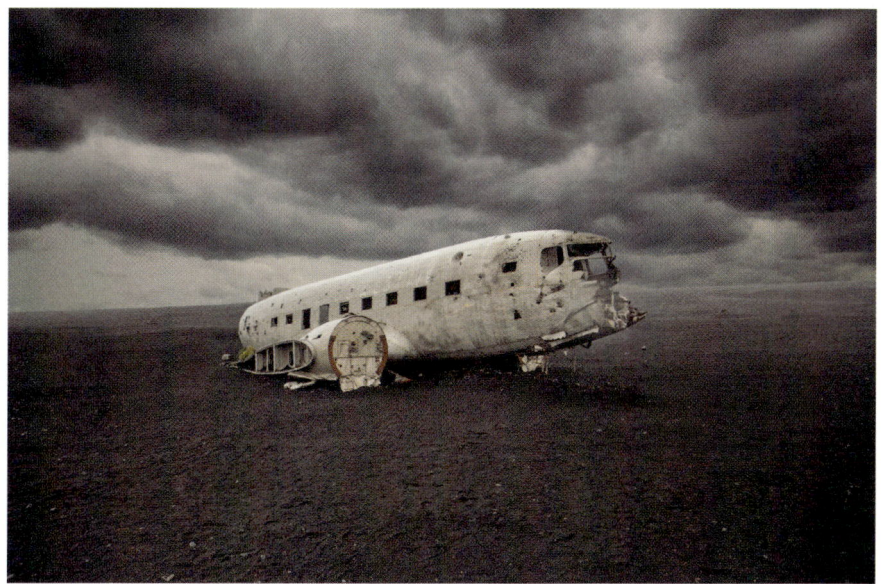

▲ *Consider whether including the background helps your image. Here, the brooding sky and volcanic sands help to create an intriguing story about this airplane, which crashed in a remote region of Iceland. Thankfully, everyone survived.*

PRO TIPS

- Try not to include too much in one frame, as it can easily create a busy and disorganized image.

- Older architecture may be entwined with plants that can really help emphasize how old or derelict it is.

- A long corridor or broken window can serve as a great compositional tool to lead a viewer's eye through an image.

- There will often be textures that can add an appealing element to a shot or even make a standalone image.

TRAVEL NOTES

- Take care when walking around derelict or rundown areas. Always be aware of your surroundings.

- Dilapidated buildings and other structures can be incredibly dangerous, so think very carefully about going inside. The building may well be unsafe or have other less obvious dangers lurking within it.

- You can find information about abandoned places online. Quite often a simple search with the location and "abandoned" will reveal some sites.

- Some historical ruins may charge an entry fee and have specific rules on photography, so check in advance.

A GRAND CANYON

At some point you will find yourself standing in front of a spectacular view that is so big and impressive that you struggle to capture it properly in camera. No matter what you try, the vastness can easily get lost when recorded as a single small image.

When this happens, creating a panoramic image that is made up of a number of smaller individual photographs could well be the answer. The aim of this assignment is to capture an immense scene as a panorama, combining your individual exposures in postproduction to create a larger, fuller, and more detailed photograph.

▼ *Scenes taken from high vantage points can offer uninterrupted views that are well suited to panoramic photographs.*

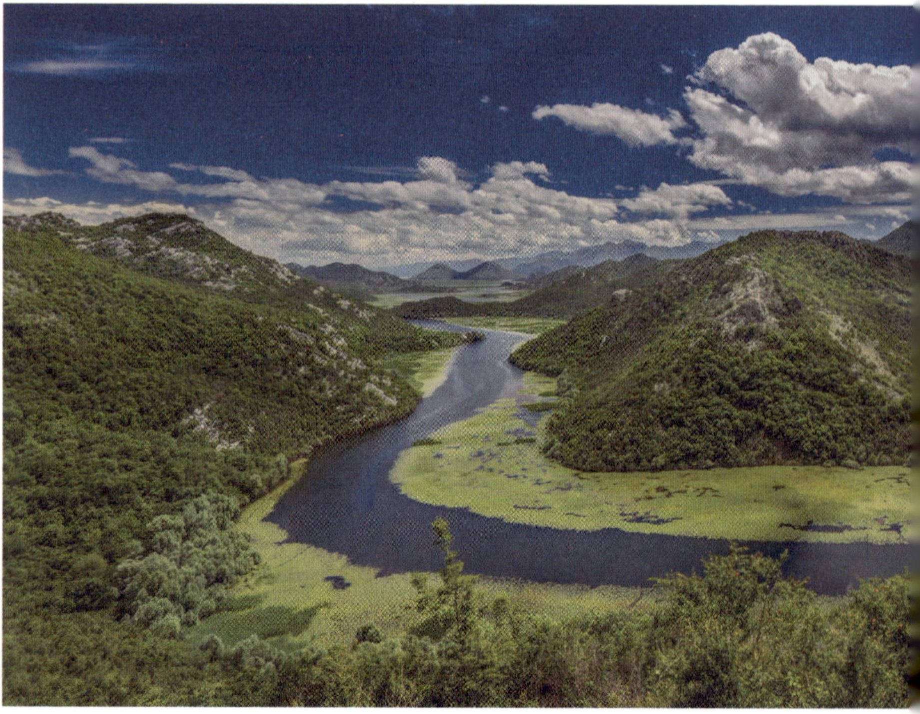

PRO TIPS

- Ensure that any filters are removed from your lens, especially a polarizer, as this will affect the sky and make it difficult to stitch the images together.

- Shoot Raw for more flexibility and dynamic range in each image. Edit your Raw files consistently before you stitch the panorama together.

- Check the sequence of images and their histograms to make sure that no areas are over- or underexposed.

- Once you have completed the panorama in postproduction, crop as necessary and remove any areas that you don't want included, or didn't have any information captured.

TECHNIQUE

1 Think about the scene and whether you want to shoot landscape (horizontal), or portrait (vertical) images. Almost all of my panoramas are shot in the portrait format so I have more information and can crop the image later.

2 It is vital to use manual settings to ensure that every image has the same focus, white balance, exposure, and depth of field. Choose the appropriate settings based on the scene as a whole, rather than for each individual image.

3 Starting at one end of your scene, take your first shot. Turn the camera to cover the next part of the scene, ensuring that you overlap each image by around 30 per cent to make stitching the panorama easier, and take another shot.

4 Keep turning the camera and shooting until you reach the opposite end of the scene you want to capture. The number of exposures you make depends on the size of the scene. Take more images to include more of the scene for better results.

5 A tripod makes it easier to ensure that the images are all level, but you should be able to do this handholding the camera with a little care—follow the horizon and use this as a guide where possible.

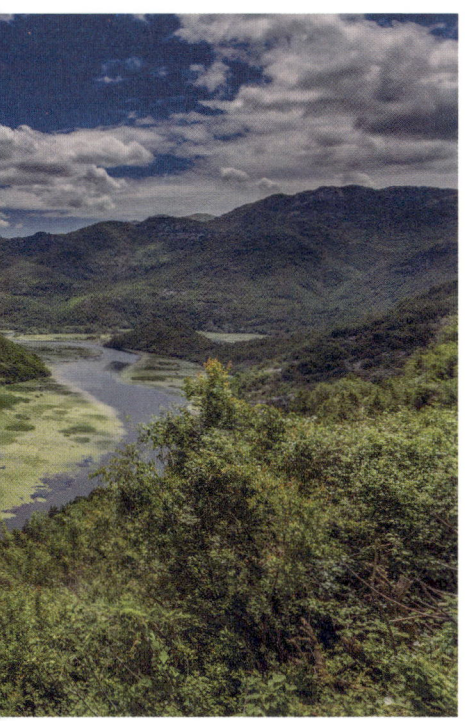

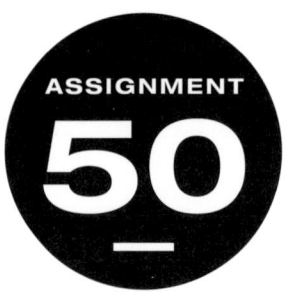

ASSIGNMENT
50

TECHNIQUE

- Your choice of focal length and viewpoint will affect the sense of depth in an image: a low viewpoint and a wideangle lens will exaggerate the sense of depth, while a high viewpoint and telephoto lens will "flatten" the depth.

- Lines can run horizontally, vertically, or diagonally through the frame, and the direction affects the viewer's journey; horizontal lines tend to "block" the viewer, vertical lines draw the eye in, and diagonals add drama.

- You don't have to use straight lines. Curved lines will take the viewer on a slower journey, while zigzags can take the eye more fully through the frame.

- Converging lines—those that meet at a specific point—are very strong, as they create a vanishing point and give your image an additional sense of depth.

- Consider shooting your image in portrait (vertical) format so you can utilize space and emphasize distance and perspective.

TRAVEL NOTES

- Leading lines are commonplace: roads, paths, shorelines, boardwalks, streams, fences, bridges, and even highlights and long shadows can create lines within an image. Nature also provides a range of strong lines when you look closely.

- Try to avoid using lines that cut across your image horizontally, such as a fence or wall, as this type of line acts as a "block" that stops the natural flow of the photograph.

- Be wary of using train tracks as leading lines, however tempting it is, unless you know for certain that the line is no longer in use.

PRO TIPS

- Don't use a leading line if it doesn't direct the viewer to a point of interest, and avoid using lines that lead the eye out of the frame.

- Lines don't have to be solid or obvious. An implied line of clouds or footprints on the sand can work well, as can the direction that someone is looking in within the frame.

ROAD TO NOWHERE

Lines are a strong and effective way to create powerful photographs. They can make your images come to life by providing a sense of depth and enhancing the illusion of a three-dimensional space. Our eyes naturally want to follow any lines we see, so "leading lines" can be used to guide your viewer's gaze toward specific parts of an image. These lines not only draw attention to one part of an image, but also create a pathway leading through the frame.

Your assignment is to produce a set of three images that utilize leading lines. You can use the lines in any way you wish—either subtly or dominating the frame—but they should take your viewer on a journey through your image. Used well they can add impact and focus, and create a strong impression of movement in the process.

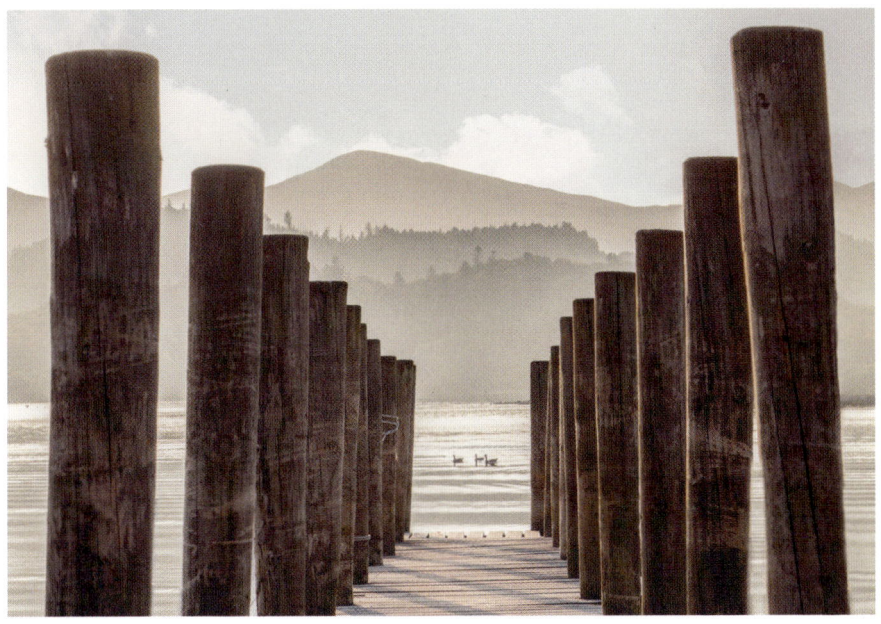

▲ *The tops and bottoms of the posts beside this wooden dock create strongly converging diagonal leading lines. These lines lead you into the frame to the three birds on the water and then upward to the mist-covered mountains.*

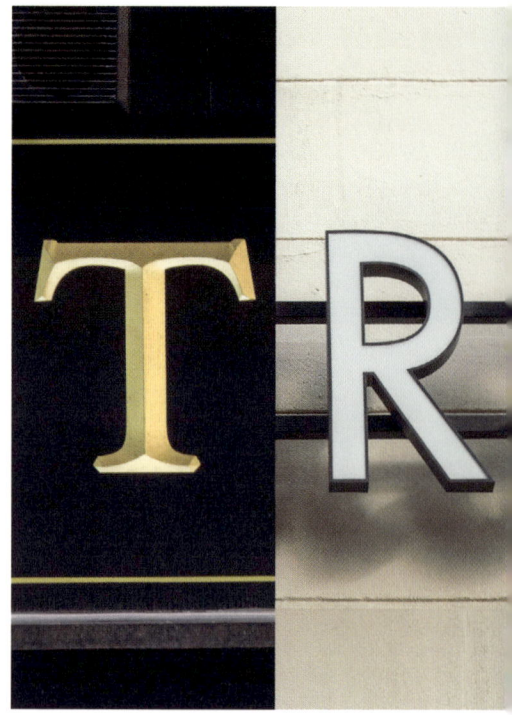

TECHNIQUE

- A telephoto lens is useful here, as it will allow you to pick out your letters from a distance.

- Keep an eye on the exposure if you are photographing illuminated letters—they may fool your camera into underexposing.

ALPHABET CITY

Every country has its own alphabet, and while some will be similar to your own, others will be different, with unique letters and characters. Even if you don't understand them, these letters and their alphabet will be all around you on your travels, in adverts, posters, storefronts, walls, the sides of buses, and so on.

Your mission is to locate stylized letters and to photograph them to create a collection that spells the name of the city or country you're traveling in. Look for intricate and unique letters that show off a mixture of local lettering styles, and don't just take all your photographs from the same location. Use this opportunity to walk, look, and explore, and if you don't already know the local alphabet take time to learn the letters or characters that make up the name of the place where you are staying.

Once you have your collection, crop each shot and combine them in postproduction to create a single image of the place name, perhaps printing the composite photograph out as a personalized souvenir of your trip.

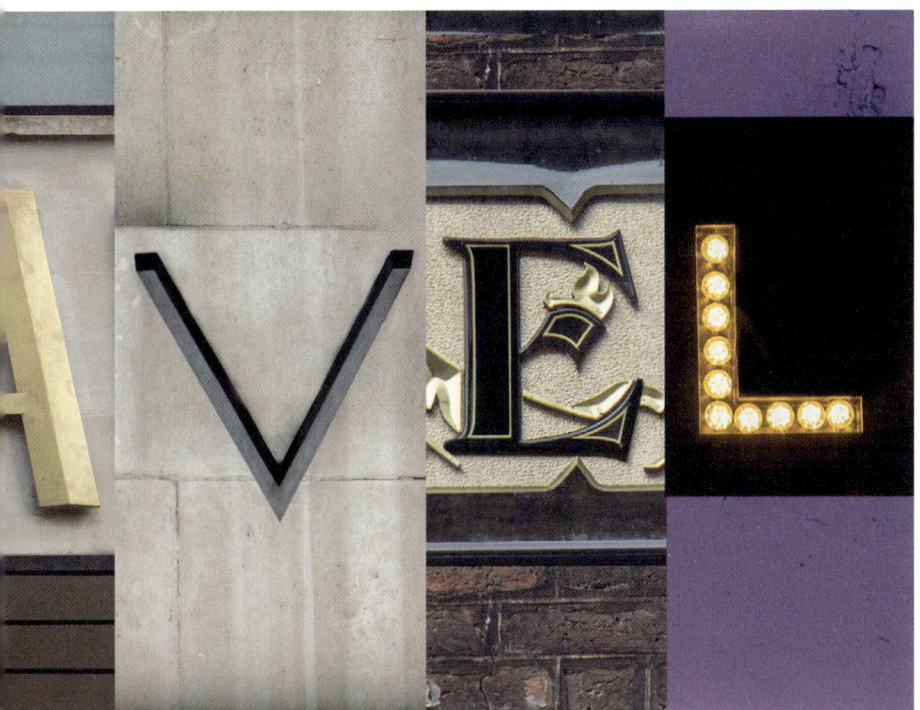

▲ *Don't be afraid to mix up colors and sizes—a splash of color can draw attention to certain letters.*

PRO TIPS

- Find a few options for each letter or character so you have a range of interesting options to choose from.

- Decide on whether you will be using lowercase or uppercase letters, or perhaps mixing the two.

- Make sure you shoot all of the letters you will need for the correct spelling!

TRAVEL NOTES

- Try to include lettering styles that relate to where you are, rather than the typefaces you see at home. The idea is to add some local style and flair to the lettering, and create a sign that represents your location.

- Different places have their own color palettes, so consider seeking out a selection of letters that use this palette so they have an additional link to your location.

- You can take the challenge a step further by finding colored letters (or backgrounds) that match the colors of the flag of the country you are in.

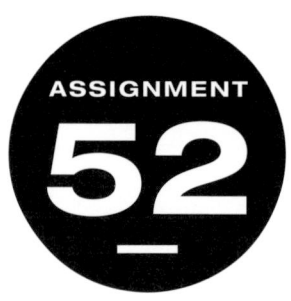

ASSIGNMENT

52

ASSIGNMENT JOURNAL

PRO TIPS

- Be selective about the images you include—only share your best work.

- Decide who you want to share your work with: do you want to limit it to friends and family, or get it out there for anyone to see?

- Printing an image can make a great gift and memento for someone you were traveling with.

TRAVEL NOTES

- A great option is to print out a few small images and stick or pin them onto a world map poster, on the country where you took the shots. Over time you can add more prints, gradually filling the poster with your global explorations.

TECHNIQUE

Online:

- Consider setting up a blog or website that lets you document your adventures with images and text. There are a number of options available, ranging from free blogs to website builders.

- If you are setting up your own website you will need to register a domain name.

- You can promote your website or blog (and link to it) through social media.

Printing:

- There are plenty of printing options, including online labs, photo stores, and in-store kiosks.

- It can be tempting to print at home, but the quality won't be as good as a professional lab unless you have a high-quality printer.

- A professional lab will be able to help with color management so your prints look the same as the image you see on your computer screen.

- Once you receive your prints, decide how you want to frame them.

CONQUER THE WORLD

So you've gone to the ends of the earth (perhaps literally!) to visit some amazing places and you've taken a whole range of images of the spectacular sights you've seen. It's all too common to put those images to one side once you return and, as time passes, perhaps they will be forgotten.

This assignment is perhaps one of the most important: don't leave your images buried on a hard drive never to be shared or seen—get them out there! There are countless options for this assignment, including setting up your own website, blog, or gallery on a photography hosting site, or sharing your travel shots online through social media accounts. Whatever option you choose, you will find that your work can be seen by friends and family, as well as strangers all over the world.

Alternatively, you could print out some of your images as small prints for a traditional photo album, or perhaps select one (or more) to print at a larger size to frame and hang on your wall. You might also choose to make a photobook of your adventures, or maybe send the results of your assignments to travel magazines. Who knows where it might lead?

▼ *A website is a great way to share your travel images, as anyone—no matter where they are in the world—can view your work. Social media is another good online option.*

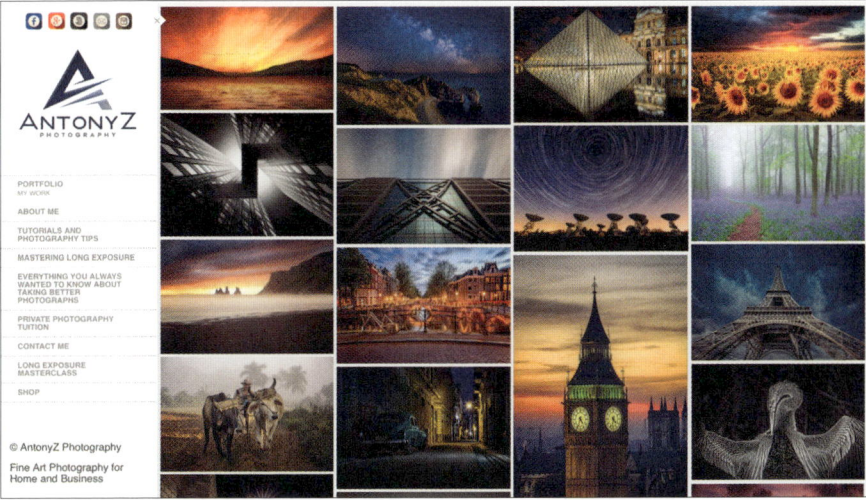

INDEX

A

abstract images 28–9, 32, 37, 67
adrenaline, creating a sense of 76–7
adventures, new 86, 94–5
alternative views 16–17, 102–3
ambiguity, in images 28–9
angle selection 22–3
animals 80–1
architecture 78–9, 116

B

black and white images 67, 98–9
blogs 124, 125
blue hours 46, 49
buildings 78–9, 116

C

cafes 42–3, 44
cities
    movement/speed 88–9
    at night 46–9, 88
    street art 92–3
clues about location 68–9
color 34–5, 100
contrasting elements 90–1

D

danger, creating a sense of 76–7
details, small 26–7

E

eating venues 42–5
epic landscapes
    emphasizing scale 60–1
    panoramic images 118–19
etiquette 25, 50, 51, 69, 81
extreme activities 76–7

F

food photography 44–5
framing subjects 58–9

G

gimmicks 56–7
golden hours 30–1
graffiti 92–3

I

iconic landmarks
    alternative views 16–17, 102–3
    replicas of 96, 97
image sequences/sets
    mixing orientations 15, 112
    panoramic images 118–19
    repeat patterns 52–3
    rephotography 18–21
    road trips 72–3
    storytelling 12–15
    travel journalism 110–13
insurance 77, 86

J

journalism 110–13
journeys, new 86, 94–5
juxtapositions 90–91

L

landmarks
    alternative views 16–17, 102–3
    replicas of 96, 97
landscapes
    emphasizing scale 60–1
    panoramic images 118–19
languages, local 25
leading lines 120–1
lettering 122–3

M

maps 86
monochrome images 67, 98–9
movement
    capturing 32–3
    cities 88–9
    water 33, 70–1
mystery, creating 10–11, 54–5, 68

N

natural world 80–1
negative space 100, 101
neon signs 49, 82, 84, 85
new locations 86, 94–5
nighttime
    architecture 78
    cities 46–9, 88
    golden hours 30–1
    reflections 9, 75
    rephotography 19, 20

P
panoramic images 118–19
patterns
  black and white images 99
  reflections 9
  repeat 52–3
  shadows 66–7
texture 108
people
  close-up 106–7
  mystery, creating 54–5
  portraits 24–5
  traditional dress 104–5
  at work 114–15
personal items 56–7
planning 86–7
portraits
  close-up 106–7
  local people 24–5
  mystery, creating 54–5
  traditional dress 104–5
  at work 114–15
postcard views 16–17, 102–3
publicizing your work 124–5

R
rain
  and cities 88
  coping with 70, 75
  reflections 9, 74, 75
reflections 8–9, 28, 48, 74, 75
  reducing 70
regional dishes 45
religion 50–51
repeat patterns 52–3
rephotography 18–21
research 86–7
road trips 72–3
ruins 116–17

S
scale, emphasizing 60–1
sequences/sets
  mixing orientations 15, 112
  panoramic images 118–19
  repeat patterns 52–3
  rephotography 18–21
  road trips 72–3
  storytelling 12–15
  travel journalism 110–13

shadows 66–67, 99, 109
sharing your work 124–5
signposting locations 68–9
signs 37, 41, 49, 68, 82–85
silhouettes 62–5
simplicity, of composition 100–1
small details 26–7
social media 124, 125
street art 92–3
sunrise/sunset 30, 31, 62–5
symmetry 8, 53, 78

T
texture 108–9
themes 36–37, 56–7
timing of shots, varying 18–21
toys 57, 96, 97
traditional dress 104–5
transportation 38–41, 72

U
unique viewpoints 22–3
urban environments
  movement/speed 88–9
  at night 46–9, 88
  street art 92–3

V
viewpoints, unique 22–3

W
water
  movement 33, 70–1
  reflections 9, 74, 75
weather conditions
  planning for 74, 75, 88
  rain 9, 70, 74, 75
  wind 9, 33, 68, 74
websites 124, 125
wildlife 80–1
wind
  capturing movement 33, 68
  and cities 88
  cloud cover 74
  reflections 9
words, images of 122–3
work images 114–15

First published 2020 by
Ammonite Press
an imprint of Guild of Master Craftsman Publications Ltd
Castle Place, 166 High Street, Lewes, East Sussex, BN7 1XU,
United Kingdom

ISBN 978 1 78145 406 0

Publisher: Jason Hook
Art director: Robin Shields
Editor: Chris Gatcum

Color reproduction by GMC Reprographics
Printed and bound in China

ACKNOWLEDGMENTS

To Thea - a new chapter begins with many roads to travel!
Once again thanks to my ever-loving parents, Shauneen
and of course to my team at Ammonite.

How was the book?
Please post your
feedback and photos:
#52AssignmentsTravel

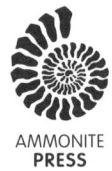

AMMONITE
PRESS

ammonitepress.com